making the most of
# small spaces

making the most of

# small spaces

by Stephen Crafti

Reprinted 2003
(The Images Publishing Group Reference Number: 505)

First published in Australia in 2002
by The Images Publishing Group Pty Ltd
ABN 89 059 734 431
6 Bastow Place, Mulgrave, Victoria, 3170
Telephone (61 3) 9561 5544
Facsimile (61 3) 9561 4860
Email: books@images.com.au
www.imagespublishinggroup.com

National Library of Australia  Cataloguing-in-Publication data

Small Spaces, Making the most of.

Includes index.
ISBN 1 876907 52 5.

Coordinating Editor: Jodie Davis
Designed by The Graphic Image Studio Pty Ltd,
Mulgrave, Australia
Film by Digital Imaging Group (DIG), Melbourne
Printed by Paramount Printing Company Limited, Hong Kong

IMAGES has included on its website a page for special
notices in relation to this and our other publications. It includes
updates in relation to the information printed in our books.
Please visit this site: www.imagespublishinggroup.com

# CONTENTS

# INTRODUCTION
## BY STEPHEN CRAFTI

This book includes apartments, townhouses, warehouses and even a prototype for a future shack. While the form of housing differs significantly, finding space is a common theme. Designing an apartment of only 50 square metres involves considerably more constraints than a townhouse three times the size. Walls are removed to increase the light and create a feeling of space. The palette of materials and finishes in the spaces are used sparingly. Where walls are used to define a space, they are designed not to meet the ceilings. A sense of the room beyond is always there. Elements designed for the space are considered for more than one function. One cupboard, used for storage, doubles as a unit to conceal the television and music system. The same cupboard might also be used to screen or divide a room.

When small does come down to 50 square metres of floor space, or a house no wider than four metres, even the smallest details become major considerations. Leaving handles off cupboards (using other mechanisms to open and close), using two-pack paint finishes to catch the sunlight and creating generous voids to overcome the small dimensions are carefully considered design options. The small spaces in this book will dispel some of the notions people have when it comes to this area of design. White walls and polished floorboards will sometimes create a feeling of more space. However, for one small townhouse, white walls were never considered. Dark charcoal brown walls allow the walls to recede and the objects within become the focus, creating a sense of space.

In many of these small spaces, one large gesture replaces several ideas that would have cluttered the space. One double-height window wall, screened with one oversized blind, is used in preference to several small porthole windows that dissect the space.

These small spaces, taken from urban and residential landscapes in Australia, are a reminder of what many talented architects and designers are capable of achieving worldwide. They are also a timely reminder of what is actually needed in a home, rather than what is simply wanted. The wish list can still be satisfied. It often just takes more thought and careful planning. As the cost of housing increases, so does the trend to living in small homes, located on smaller sites. The standard quarter acre block, which includes a three-bedroom house and rolling lawn, is not always possible, or even desired. The idea of living in a small space in the city or on the fringe may be more appealing, particularly for those with smaller sized families. The spaces might be small, but the skills used to rework these spaces are immense. When you realise that some of the spaces featured in this book are no larger than someone's back veranda, the importance of good design is immediately visible.

These small spaces are
a reminder of what many
talented architects and
designers are capable
of achieving...

# Just Over Three Metres Wide!

## Allen Jack + Cottier Architects
Photography: Max Dupain

There would not be too many homes that are just over three metres in width, but this four-level home makes up the space with its verticality. An inner-city Victorian terrace, it was in a derelict condition when architect Peter Stronach of Allen Jack + Cottier Architects first inspected the site. Given the condition it was in, it is not surprising the brief was to virtually rebuild the terrace, with new bathrooms, kitchen, living space and as much light as possible.

The design centres on opening the restricted volume of the house vertically, using several void spaces to create a feeling of spaciousness. Attracting light from rear roof windows and glazed full-length doors was crucial to the reworking of the home. The two-storey terrace was completely gutted to accommodate three new levels. The dining and kitchen areas are found at entry level, living and study areas on the middle level and a bedroom and bathroom were designed for the top level. The voids created on the second and third levels add a feeling of vertical space and allow the natural light to penetrate well into the interior.

While the interior of this home features pure white walls, the exterior features a whimsical colour scheme of mauves and pinks. Not the traditional heritage scheme, the colours were designed to poke fun at local planning authorities. 'There were so many delays in getting this project through. The local Council objected to the changes on the basis of aesthetics and taste', says Stronach. Finding anything that would be objectionable in this delightful home would be difficult. Moving through the open and light spaces, the width of the terrace is no longer an issue.

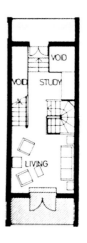

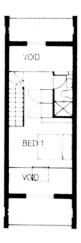

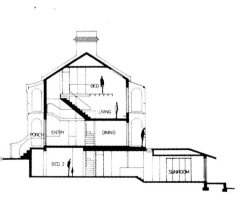

# SCALE AND RHYTHM

## ALLEN JACK + COTTIER ARCHITECTS

Photography: Tony Spragg

These narrow townhouses evoke forms typical of the 19th-century terrace. However, once through the front door, any remnant of the past is left behind. Unlike traditional terrace homes, where rooms are placed at each turn of the staircase, the rooms in these homes are designed in a scissor shape. Designed by architect Peter Stronach of Allen Jack + Cottier Architects, the townhouses feature a series of split-level sections. The living areas on the entry level are only a few steps away from the dining area above. A similar distance also separates the three bedrooms on the levels above. To create a feeling of space in the townhouse, the design includes slightly higher ceilings for the living spaces (3 metres), than for the bedrooms.

While each townhouse has its own private rear garden, they also include a generous terrace area for alfresco dining. As the townhouses are relatively narrow, like most 19th-century terraces, solid and continuous walls are not used in the interior. A feature timber wall is used to define the kitchen. However, instead of designing a solid wall, Stronach opened the kitchen to the stairwell, this space doubling as a servery if required. To keep the staircase as transparent as possible, Stronach relied on a solid stainless steel handrail and steel wiring.

Due to the slope of the land, parking is provided for the 13 two- and three-storey homes below street level. Placing the car parking below street level allows the open spaces to be used for recreation. With cars buried below the site, there is a continuous flow to the streetscape.

# ANYTHING IS POSSIBLE

## ALSOCAN ARCHITECTS

Photography: Andrew Morant & David Beynon

Architects David Beynon and Jane McDougall of Alsocan Architects bought this small terrace with the intention of using it as a home and office. The terrace, with its 'shotgun' corridor down one side, had the usual configuration of external rooms – separate bathroom, laundry and toilet.

As a means of developing a profile to the street, the small front garden was redesigned to include extra space for the front office. Two separate entrances were also designed, one for the office, the other for the dwelling. 'We really needed to create the feeling of going home after work and to give the living space a sense of seclusion from the busy street', Beynon says. The two front rooms were retained for the practice, but the north-facing kitchen and outbuildings were removed.

Through the Victorian-style front door, the original polished floorboards give way to polished concrete. 'This new fin wall allows more light to enter the passage. It acts as an interlocking mechanism between the two styles', Beynon says. Into the separate living area, the curved hoop pine wall is directed towards the light. The mezzanine bedroom remains partially obscured from below.

The boat-like structure, which contains the bedroom, also acts as the canopy for the kitchen. The architects felt it was important to keep many of the quirky features that had been added to the terrace by the previous owners. The old kitchen cupboards were retained but repainted in candy pinks and mint greens. A remodelled 1950s stove and oven takes pride of place in the kitchen, along with a table setting from the same period.

The house is about creating a feeling of space. As Beynon explains: 'This room is just over three metres wide, but by slanting this dividing wall (containing the bathroom and laundry), the room appears much larger'. If you're wondering about the name, Alsocan goes back to the time David and Jane were working in Singapore. As McDougall says, 'Every time we were asked if a task was possible, the reply would be 'also can', meaning anything was possible'.

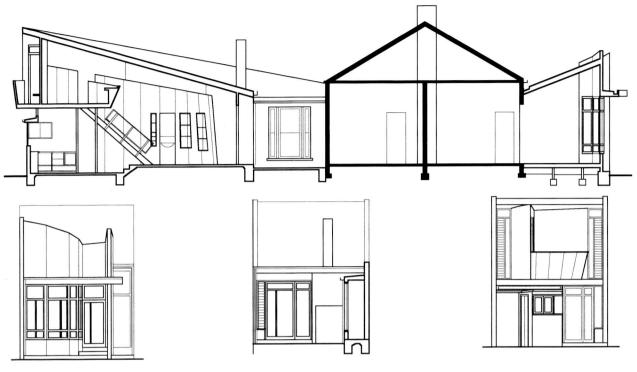

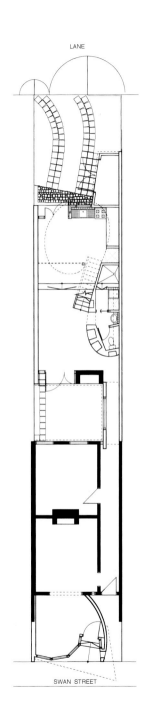

LANE

SWAN STREET

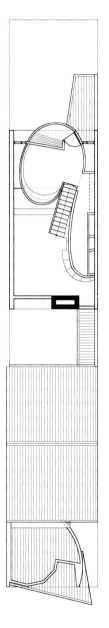

# PUSHING THE ENVELOPE
## b.e.ARCHITECTURE
Photography: Trevor Mein

Located in a laneway, the main attribute of this small site was the privacy it afforded. For b.e.Architecture, who were commissioned to design a new house on the site, the brief was challenging. However, even the request for two tandem parking spaces on the site did not cause them alarm. 'We tend to make the problems or constraints part of the solution. It's the way we work', says designer Broderick Ely of b.e.Architecture.

Even though the site might appear like an island, the act of pushing the envelope to the boundaries is still tempered by regulations. 'Even if you can't see the house from the street, issues such as overshadowing neighbouring properties affect the design'. High walls surround the home (2.4 metres in height) and floor-to-ceiling glass windows and doors look out towards the pond, a substitute for the suburban back lawn. 'The pond is less than a metre wide, but it creates an important vista on a narrow site. You would have felt closed in with planting', Ely says. Even though the kitchen and living area is spacious, the custom-made joinery eliminates the need to furnish the house with freestanding pieces.

'The joinery acts as the walls and maximises the spaces in the home. For a site this wide (approximately 5 metres), it was important to eliminate corridors where possible', Ely explains.

Instead of creating a warren of rooms, b.e.Architecture designed fewer continuous open spaces. Constructed in concrete, timber and stone, the house has a monumental feel. 'Everything is oversized and expansive for such a small block', Ely says. The main bedroom, with its floor-to-ceiling windows, was designed to benefit from its private domain. When the large sliding windows/doors are pulled back, the boundaries between the interior and exterior become blurred. The elevated window ledge, which doubles as seating, further eliminates the need for extra furniture and frees up the space.

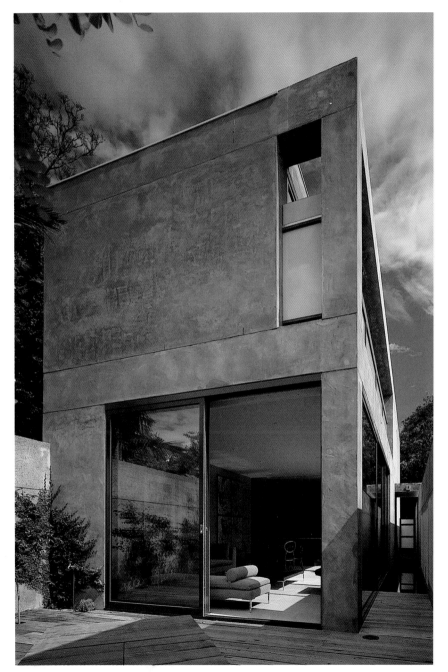

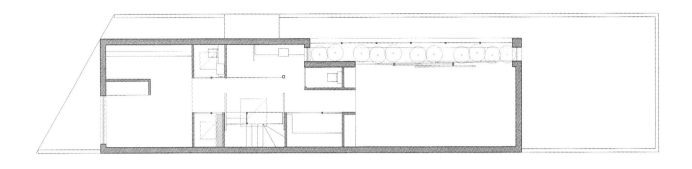

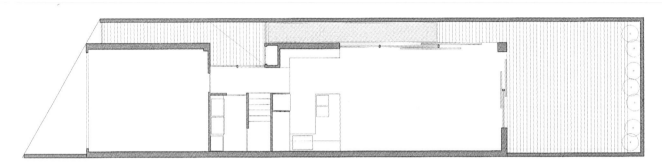

# GOING VERTICAL
## BBP ARCHITECTS
Photography: Christopher Ott

'You mightn't have the width, but you still have the height', says architect David Balestra-Pimpini of BBP Architects. For a small single-fronted terrace, the width of the terrace was fixed. However, there was scope on the vertical level.

'The principal aim of this design was to create as much living space as possible, as well as maximising the natural light throughout the residence', Balestra-Pimpini says. While the original front rooms were retained, the series of lean-tos that were added to the home over the years were removed. To activate the space (with light and ventilation), a glass window wall approximately five metres in height was designed for the rear elevation. 'The wall brings in the morning light and gives the new space a sense of volume. It comes as a surprise after leaving the narrow passage running along the front of the house', he adds.

The new addition, which includes the bathroom, laundry, sitting room, dining area and kitchen, also manages to include a mezzanine study area, accessed by a ladder. 'Most terraces cover between 70–80 per cent of the site. Our approach was to carve out an internal space and to make an important visual connection to the rear garden', he says. The large glass sliding door to the back garden blurs the division between the interior and exterior spaces. The rear courtyard garden now acts as an extension to the living space.

While the mezzanine above creates additional floor space in the home, it also creates a division between the dining and lounge areas. The lowered ceiling under the mezzanine also accentuates the generous voids in the space. A feeling of space was also created in the galley-style kitchen, which is open to the living areas. Starting from the fridge to the pantry, the cupboards have been cleverly 'stepped in' to accentuate the size of the kitchen.

'With most of our projects, we try to design a fairly neutral canvas. The space and the light are crucial to the design. It is then up to the clients to personalise the space to suit their needs', Balestra-Pimpini says. From the street, with its high steel front fence, the terrace suggests a dark, almost forbidding home. However, past the front door, it does not take long to appreciate its other side.

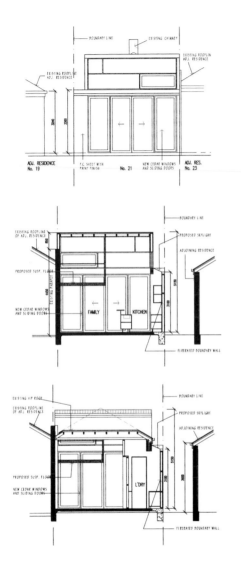

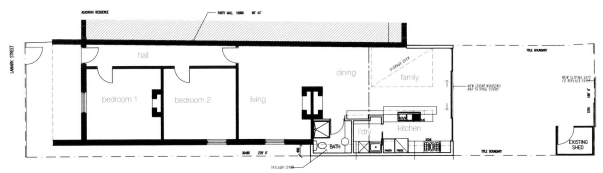

# THE ILLUSION OF SPACE
## BURLEY KATON HALLIDAY
Photography: Sharrin Rees

For this small block of only 12 apartments, the architects Burley Katon Halliday pushed the building's envelope to its limit. With each apartment measuring approximately 54 square metres, creating a sense of space was a challenge. 'Apartments can feel oppressive at that size', says architect David Katon, one of the firm's directors.

With an identical layout for each apartment, the façade of the building is symmetrical, six apartments on either side of the central staircase. Located in an industrial area, the cues for the design came in part from the neighbouring factories. The louvred bank of windows that extends over two levels is reminiscent of some of the louvred factory windows nearby. 'The floors are polished concrete and the walls are crudely bagged. They are not particularly sharp finishes. It's more the language of the area', Katon says.

While the footprint of each apartment is relatively small, the gestures within are comparatively large. The louvred windows in each apartment are approximately 4.5 metres in height (creating light and ventilation). The volume of the vertical space more than compensates for the limited floor area. 'We kept everything simple, from the detailing to the amount of joinery', Katon says.

One large industrial light on the wall was chosen instead of a ceiling dotted with halogen lights. One large retractable blind over the entire window creates a larger gesture, rather than a series of curtains. In the same way, there is one sweep of cupboards in the kitchen.

Upstairs, the mezzanine bedroom (which includes the bathroom and laundry), was left open. Encased by a stainless steel balustrade and a steel handrail, the two levels can both enjoy the light and the ventilation. 'The blinds filter the view when privacy is required. When they are down, you can just see the outlines of the surrounding buildings', Katon says. Instead of a series of small private balconies, Burley Katon Halliday designed one large roof-top terrace. 'The whole roof is like one large timber deck. A portion is protected with a roof. Two thirds is open to the sky. It meant that everyone had more outdoor space and better views', he says.

The apartments pulsate with activity. 'If you don't have the floor space, you need to compensate with volume', Katon says. 'It's a matter of keeping things fairly simple and uncluttered'.

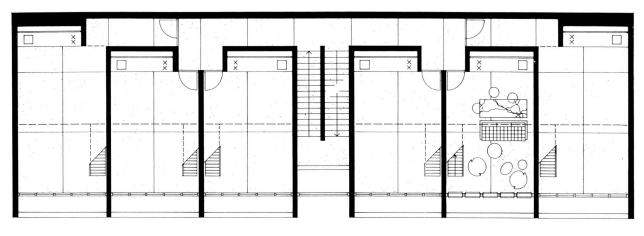

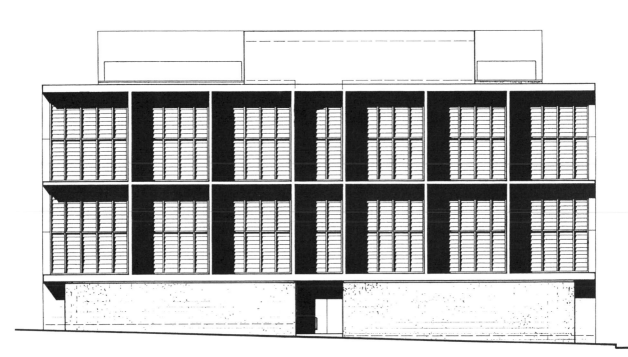

# THE CORNER STORE

CHERYL CAMERON
Photography: Sarah Matray

Belonging to the same family for nearly fifty years, this home was originally the local corner store. 'The store had been divided up to include at least six bedrooms', says designer Cheryl Cameron, who recently removed its layered past. 'The rooms were dark. Most of the walls were finished in a faux timber laminex', she adds.

Six bedrooms were not part of the brief when Cameron redesigned this home. Two bedrooms and spacious living areas certainly were. While Cameron kept the exterior relatively intact, she made some changes to the entry. 'I sealed up the original front door - which would have led to the store - and used the side door as the main entrance. I don't like living spaces to feel as though they were part of the corridor', she says. Internal walls were removed to create both light and spacious rooms. Instead of a series of doorways that dissect the space, Cameron designed a series of diagonal nib walls. Angled towards the rear garden, the walls act as reflective panels for the natural light. 'I generally prefer to have all-white walls. The light creates the subtle tones, from shade to half-light. In a small space, I generally try and minimise the range of materials and colours'.

As the kitchen was designed as part of one of the three living areas, it was not treated in the traditional manner. Sculptural cubes substitute for overhead kitchen cupboards. The cupboards were designed as a piece of furniture in a living room. They are cantilevered above the floor to create a lighter feel. A new staircase was designed to replace the worn timber staircase that existed. With its open treads, light is able to filter into the home's darkest nook. The dark passage, which included a fireplace, has been redesigned for the downstairs bathroom.

As Cameron says, 'I've unified the small spaces. The feeling of space comes from the light and the pure white walls. It is almost monastic in its simplicity. The light's been manipulated in every possible way. White planes of glass have been inserted into light boxes and the diagonal wall planes reflect the light'. While the house now has considerably fewer rooms, the quality of the spaces is now significantly greater.

# FINDING SPACE
## CHRISTOPHER DE CAMPO
## ARCHITECTS
Photography: John Gollings

Books are piled on chairs. Miniature tea sets frame the kitchen sink and dollhouses are carefully arranged on the polished concrete floors. Finding the four-poster bed or the bathroom among the paintings and armoires is not unlike following a goat's trail through an exotic mountainous location. For artist Mirka Mora, the space that she uses as both a studio and a home, is as fascinating as Mora's well-documented life.

This large one-room apartment forms part of a larger development. Designed by Christopher de Campo Architects, the building includes the William Mora Gallery and a number of apartments. Designed on a small site, 16 metres x 32 metres, the brief to Christopher de Campo was to integrate both commercial and domestic functions within the one building.

Mirka's apartment, which is located on the first floor, consists of one large space. Instead of walls defining spaces within, books, wardrobes, shelves and objects create the parameters. The many aisles of books replace the singular passage and lead in numerous directions, to the kitchen sink or to the studio. The only structural division is the outline of a staircase leading to the apartments above. 'I like to see the whole place and be able to assess my work.

I did not want divisions and I did not want to screen the view with curtains. I do not like doors [the bathroom was designed with mirrors and translucent glass panels]', Mirka says. In contrast to the dark studio where she previously worked, the light has given Mirka a new sense of clarity. 'I can feel the change even in the way I use paint. It's affected the way I move the colours around', she adds.

The home feels like a gallery. Alternatively, the William Mora Gallery feels as welcoming as a home. The gallery is used for the occasional dinner party and then acts as a dining room. 'The building is not strictly defined. It is about freely moving into the spaces and being able to have privacy should it be required', de Campo says. While the building is not strictly carved up, the zincalum and colour bond façade outlines the functions within. 'The ribbed profile of the zincalum defines William's large family apartment and his office. The horizontal colour bond identifies the other apartments from the street', he says.

Even though things appear chaotic in the apartment, they can always be found. As Mirka says, 'Fred [her grandson, who lives in the same building] loves exploring the studio. I think that he knows the place better than me'.

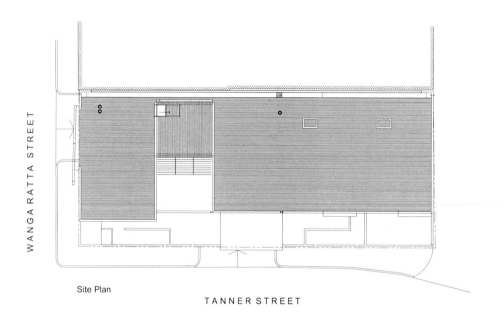

Site Plan

WANGARATTA STREET

TANNER STREET

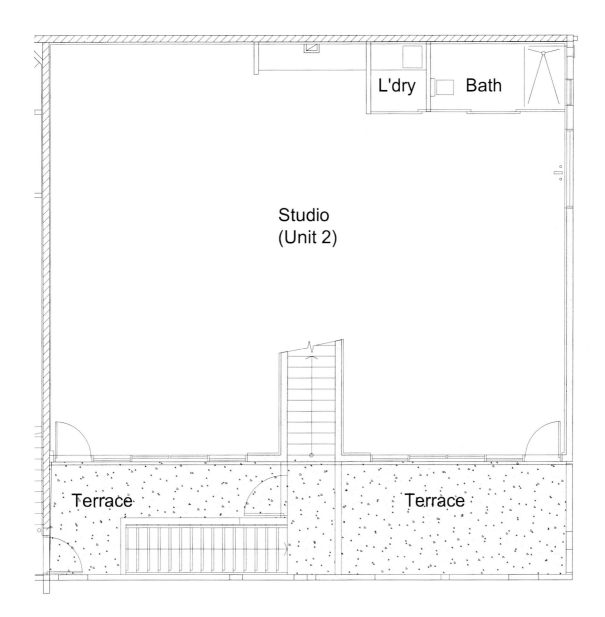

L'dry

Bath

Studio
(Unit 2)

Terrace

Terrace

# DOWNSIZING
## CRACKNELL & LONERGAN ARCHITECTS
Photography: Simon Kenny

Originally built in the 1860s, this home was lived in by a family of six in the 1940s. Built with only two rooms downstairs and one room upstairs, it is difficult to reconcile the number of people with the spaces provided. However, when the new owners of this home moved in, the house had already been converted into an office.

'The entire house, including the rear terrace, is only about 50 square metres', say architects Julie Cracknell and Peter Lonergan, who purchased the house for their own home. When the couple purchased the house, the backyard was completely lined with quarry tiles. The kitchen and bathroom were simply tacked on the back in a fibro structure. 'It was only a step from the shower to the stove', Cracknell says. While Cracknell & Lonergan Architects didn't significantly increase the floor space of the home, they did make the space more functional. 'We relocated the front door to the side of the house. It made the front room useable instead of it being treated as a passageway'.

A new kitchen was designed for the space, as was a new dining room and lounge nook. The kitchen, which acts as the spine of the home, features the usual bank of cupboards lined with printed floral laminex.

The design is partially about our childhood memories from the 1950s. There is a certain holiday house feel to the design, particularly with the links to the outside spaces', Cracknell says. 'We were inspired by Japanese design and the work of architects such as Carlo Scarpa, who knows how to integrate the new with the original'. While the original walls were left intact, Cracknell & Lonergan designed a new curved roof for the living spaces. The vaulted ceiling, made of hoop pine, creates a sense of space and height.

While the main bedroom upstairs was sufficient for two, the original lean-to bathroom was inadequate. The roof space was used to create the new bathroom. When the timber screens are kept open, a feeling of bathing outdoors is created. 'There is quite a strong Balinese feel to the design. In summer there is a continual breeze', Cracknell says. Trying to imagine a family of six in this home is difficult. Even by today's standards, the 50-square-metre home is considered small. However, with greater access to the garden and functional design features, this home feels considerably larger than its original imprint.

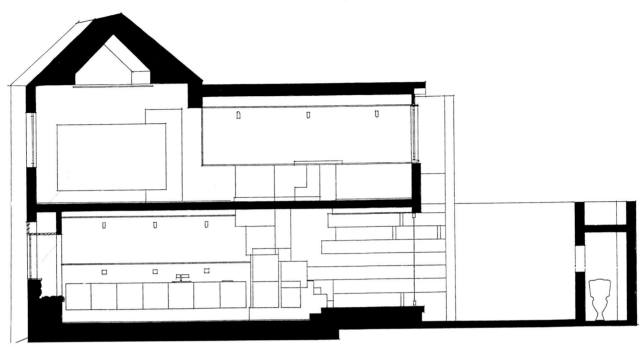

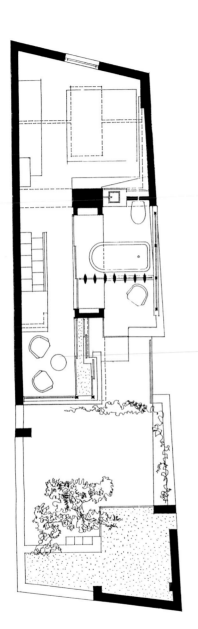

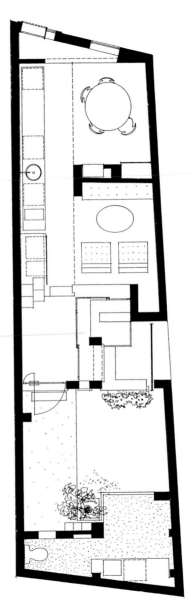

# A CONSERVATORY
## SUZANNE DANCE
### Photography: Andrew Lecky

Ornate iron lacework and a decorative parapet have seduced many people into purchasing Victorian terrace homes. After the seduction, however, comes the realisation that many of these homes require considerable work. Owned by the same family for 70 years, this house had been boarded up and left empty for the last 15 years, which added to the attention required.

When architect Suzanne Dance first inspected the home, the rear elevation was little more than a series of makeshift rooms that had been added over the decades. The result was a dark interior with no link to the rear garden. The solution was to create a new conservatory with floor-to-ceiling glass windows. A large steel bay window hovers under a new pergola, while a smaller version was designed for the upstairs bedroom. 'The large bay window [2.5 metres x 2.5 metres] is reminiscent of a Victorian conservatory. Originally there were no windows directed towards the light and there was no connection to the backyard', Dance says. As the terrace was so intact, Dance endeavoured to retain as much of the original home as possible. 'I prefer to work in a continuous way, in a sense like a temporary custodian. I prefer to leave the bare bones rather than obliterating them'.

However, when it came to designing the new kitchen and conservatory, both the architect and the client were not afraid to move forward.

The external steel pergola, which is linked to the conservatory, creates a sense of space as it reaches towards the rear boundary. Instead of a small archway, typical of the Victorian period, Dance designed the sunroom and conservatory as one room, with the existing walls taken back as far as possible. Light streams into the kitchen and living areas and there are now garden views. A light touch was also applied when it came to designing the kitchen. There is a simple rhythm to the kitchen cupboards, which draws attention to the high ceilings, rather than its elongated profile. As a counterpoint to the decorative plasterwork, Dance's renovation is graphic and simple. Whether it is the steel grid-like lines of the conservatory or the carefully articulated lines of the new joinery, the renovation appears spacious. It is only a small addition to the home, but creates a strong and lasting gesture in the process.

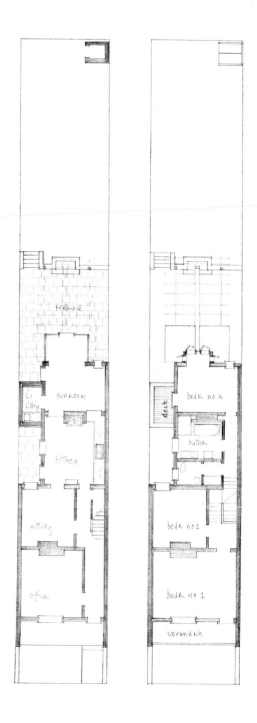

# A GARDEN ROOM

## SUZANNE DANCE

Photography: Andrew Lecky

This small weatherboard home, built at the turn of the 20th century, felt smaller than it actually was. Double-fronted and with three bedrooms, it did not lack amenities. However, with its long central passage and restricted views, the house appeared relatively small. The close proximity of the exterior walls to the side boundaries also increased the sense of enclosure.

As a way of allowing the site to 'breathe', architect Suzanne Dance set back the new garden room from the side boundaries. By creating more generous setbacks for the new addition, views from the existing home were achieved. Instead of mimicking the original style, Dance was inspired by the home's form. 'The addition is at once similar to and different from the existing home. The new corrugated steel hip roof echoes the hip roof of the original house. However, the materials and detailing, such as the corrugated steel walls and inverted rolled eaves, emphasise the pavilion as an independent object', Dance says. While the style of the garden room is independent, the rolled eaves in particular recall the fluid lines of the art nouveau period at the turn of the century, when the house was built.

With full-length doors to the garden, both the views and the light accentuate the size of the living room. As a way of drawing in a continual stream of light, Dance also designed a series of highlight windows to frame the new addition. While the adjacent galley-style kitchen is relatively narrow, Dance included in the design a large 'picture window' that doubles as a servery to the garden room. With access to the new room via a kinked and narrow passageway, entering the new wing is a dramatic contrast. 'Up to that point, the space is fairly compressed. Through the diagonal passage, the new space is loftier and much lighter. It is almost has if a weight has been lifted off your shoulders', Dance says.

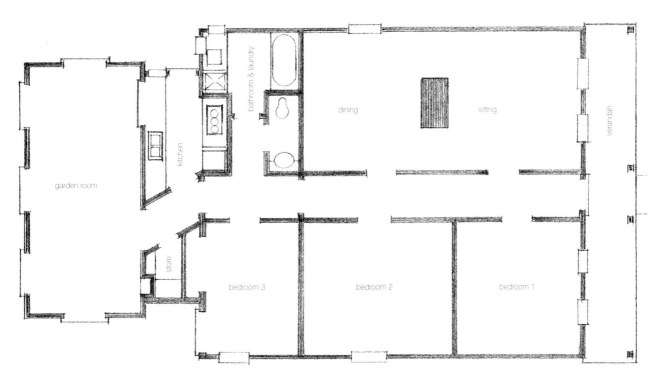

garden room

kitchen

bathroom & laundry

dining

sitting

verandah

store

bedroom 3

bedroom 2

bedroom 1

# New Life for a Small Terrace

## DAVID LUCK ARCHITECTURE

Interior Designer: Dorothy De Guara
Photography: Trevor Mein

The most lasting symbol of Victoriana is the iron lacework across the front veranda. However, once through the front door to this home, it would be difficult finding any other remnant from the past. This small terrace home was originally divided in the traditional way, formal rooms at the front with a kitchen at the rear. However, for the owner Dorothy De Guara, an interior designer, and architect David Luck, who renovated the terrace, the past was history.

Sheaths of glass that substitute for traditional lace curtains create the first signal that modernity is just behind the front door. For De Guara and Luck, who worked together on this project, the initial idea was to retain the two front rooms. 'It's the usual approach for terraces, with a courtyard acting as a light well in the middle. We didn't want any walls or divisions in the house. First we eliminated the two front rooms, then the courtyard', Luck says. 'Most architects can provide space and light in a terrace. It is also important to provide an emotional content to the space', he adds.

As the house (which is just over four metres wide) is located in a heritage area, the façade was fully retained. However, within the building there is no distinction between the old and the new. 'It is one supreme renovation', says Luck. With the relocation of the bedrooms to upstairs, the kitchen and living areas are in full view from the front door. 'I wanted to be able to appreciate the full proportions of the house, so your eyes skim over the furniture and the reflective glass within', De Guara says. 'I designed the furniture with Andre Loze and we concentrated on fewer pieces. The four dining room bench chairs comfortably sit eight', she adds.

One of the reasons the renovation works so successfully is the extraordinary level of detail. As part of the brief was to 'make the kitchen fade', Luck designed a ten-metre-long kitchen island bench made of sandstone. With all the kitchen appliances concealed behind stainless steel cupboards, the kitchen resembles solid basalt rock. Instead of turned polished wooden balustrades, seen in many terraces, Luck designed two staircases in the form of cantilevered steel plates, placed behind glass screens. As Luck says, 'A glass box at the back does not have to be the only solution. It is sometimes frustrating to join the 'two-headed beast' - the old and the new - and having the two styles compete with each other'.

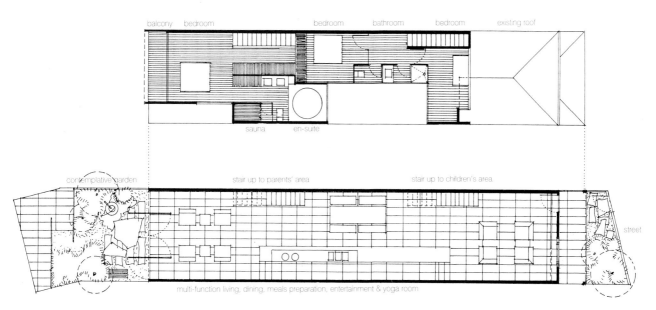

balcony  bedroom                 bedroom    bathroom    bedroom        existing roof

sauna      en-suite

contemplative garden      stair up to parents' area        stair up to children's area

street

multi-function living, dining, meals preparation, entertainment & yoga room

# A BOATSHED
## DESIGN KING COMPANY
Photography: Jon King

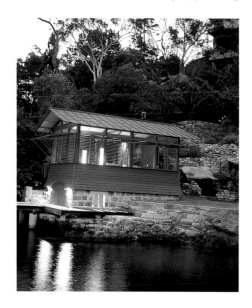

Accessible via a long and steep path and hidden from view, this small boatshed is a five-minute walk from the main house. Designed by architect Jon King of the Design King Company, the small shed came as an additional brief while the architect was renovating the owner's house.

'The brief for the boatshed was fairly open. They wanted something that would act as a base when visitors arrived by boat - the site looks out over a harbour', King says. However, what was seen initially as a place to simply store a boat and an arrival point for visitors has quickly become the focus of the property. With only a limited amount of space, approximately 6.5 metres by 3.5 metres, the footprint was limited. King was able to excavate the site to at least create a double-storey structure, using the lower level to house the boat and as an area for wine storage and the upper level for additional living space.

Although the actual boatshed is small, the views surrounding the shed are extensive. To work with such breathtaking views, King's design was kept simple. 'There are no internal walls and the kitchen was treated like a piece of joinery. The sleeping arrangements are also simple. The built-in lounges double as beds. The capacity is about six', says King.

The oregon timber shutters filter the light, or can be placed horizontally to create a seamless view of the harbour. 'It is quite secluded down here. The site is sheltered and has its own sub-climate. In winter, it is a suntrap', he says.

All the materials for the boatshed were selected for their durability. The stone for the base was found on site, while the hardwood timber was brought in by boat. While the structure is small, the detail was magnified. 'The joints were interlocked with plywood and connected with stainless steel screws. Plywood is also used to brace the building in the roof and below the sills which act as both the lining and the structure', King says.

For many occasions, visitors don't have to make their way up the steep path to the house. The table is set and dining is by the water. For the owners, who have teenaged children, the boatshed is ideal for their parties and sleepovers. 'The dining room table can be pushed to one side and a few extra mattresses can be laid on the floor. It is quite a simple building. It is really about enjoying the views'.

**Timber Decking**
Kiln Dried Blackbutt

**Timber Supplier**
Harper Timber

**Timber Shutters**
Oregon (made by Mandalong Woodworking)

**Hardwood Finish**
Feast Watson Deck Oil

**Floor Finish**
Feast Watson Floor Seal

**Weatherboard and Shutter Finish**
Taubmans Sunproof 'Rocky'

**Roof**
Copper (By Copperform)

**Lighting**
JSB

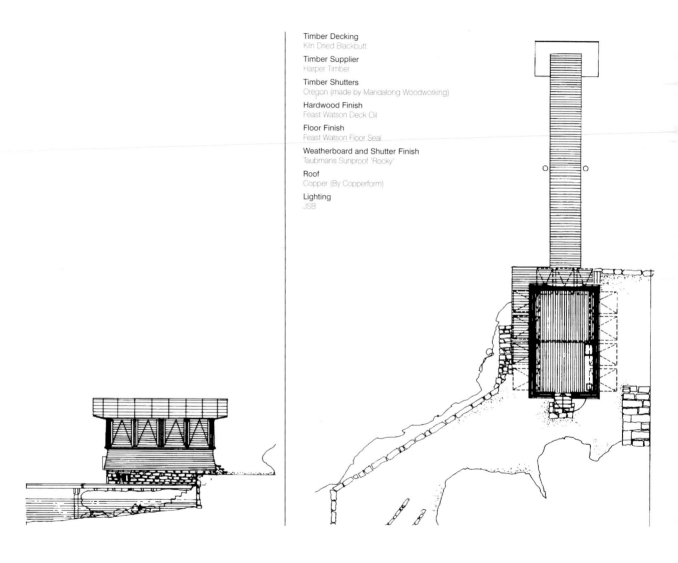

# A LITTLE GEM
## FORM FOLLOWS FUNCTION
Photography: Petrina Tinslay

This compact seven square maisonette is a fine example of a place where every millimetre counts. Named 'Montrose', the maisonette was originally designed by architect Neville Gruzman in 1955. When designers Trudi Scrymgour and Keith Glover of Form Follows Function were commissioned to redesign the landmark building, they were keen to retain its integrity.

Using materials reminiscent of the post-war period, the duo approached the design with sensitivity. 'We used reflective materials such as colour-backed glass in the kitchen, and simply laminated the front cupboards. We really used elements that were already there. The perforated plywood lighting pelmets were reinstated', says Scrymgour. In the bedroom, study and open living area, the spaces are relatively deceptive due to the large floor-to-ceiling window walls. 'The appeal of many apartments of this vintage is that they are light, have high ceilings and are usually open plan. It is what people are looking for now', she says. However, instead of simply restoring this Gruzman classic, new decorative elements, such as a graphic laminate mural, were included. The aubergine, black and white feature wall is one of the few bold elements in the space.

The kitchen, which forms part of the central column, is partially concealed behind the laminate wall. Like a drawer that can be opened when things are needed, the kitchen appliances, such as the pantry and refrigerator, are only revealed when needed. While the materials in the kitchen are new, they were carefully selected to evoke the period; glass mosaic tiles, terrazzo bench tops, laminate cabinets, colour-backed glass and stainless steel fittings.

As Scrymgour says, 'The renovation focuses on producing an interior to continue the clarity and form of the external envelope. The rectilinear strength of the space was extended by opening the existing kitchen to create one expansive space'. The partially louvered windows also create a continuous circulation of air, eliminating the problem of heat caused by so many glazed windows.

The Montrose maisonette reflects the confidence and optimism of the post-war era. Nearly half a century later, this home still has a sharp and contemporary edge.

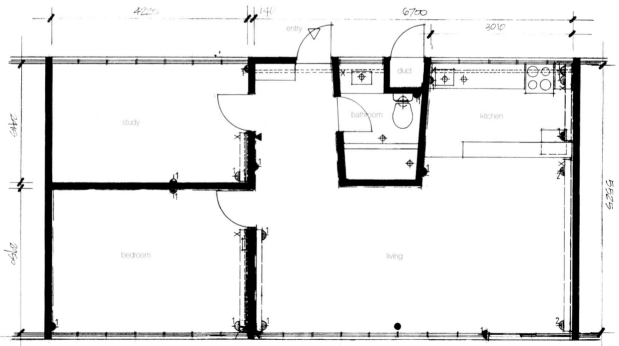

study

bedroom

entry

bathroom

duct

kitchen

living

4220

140

6700

3010

# WEDGED IN
## HARMER ARCHITECTURE
Photography: Trevor Mein

A small wedge-shaped piece of ground behind an architect's office remained idle for years. Measuring approximately 55 square metres, the land produced a dilemma for the architect: subdivide and sell or redevelop? With its unusual shape and miniscule proportions (3.5 metres at its widest end tapering down to 1.9 metres), it's not surprising that the architect, Philip Harmer, deliberated for a number of years.

The house that emerged from these deliberations has been termed 'The Wedge' by the locals, and covers approximately eighty per cent of the site. Made of concrete with a rubber roof, it is well anchored into the street. Only the cantilevered windows on the first floor spill onto the footpath. The black rubber membrane, which is stretched over the roof, eliminates the need for bulky tiles.

Downstairs, the bedroom and home office draw light from the rear yard of Harmer's own practice. On the opposite side of the staircase, the main bathroom is dependent on indirect lighting. This spacious bathroom, with its floor-to-ceiling tiles, could be in any large suburban home.

As space was a precious commodity, Harmer used the joinery to substitute for some of the furniture. A cantilevered angular tabletop runs the length of the kitchen cabinets.

The stove and sink are cleverly inserted into the narrowest point of the wedge. To make the space feel larger, a segment of the floor was removed and inserted with toughened glass. With views to the entrance below, the space takes on grander proportions. While there is insufficient space for a separate dining room, Harmer was able to include a relatively spacious lounge area.

'The Wedge' does not have off-street car parking or a front lawn lined with standard roses. However, once through the front door and up the staircase, the dimensions are surprisingly spacious. It is only by looking through the windows to the footpath below that the true dimensions of this house can be fully appreciated. As Harmer says, 'The project really challenged the notion of space and dimension. It also illustrates that you can live quite comfortably with a minimum of things'.

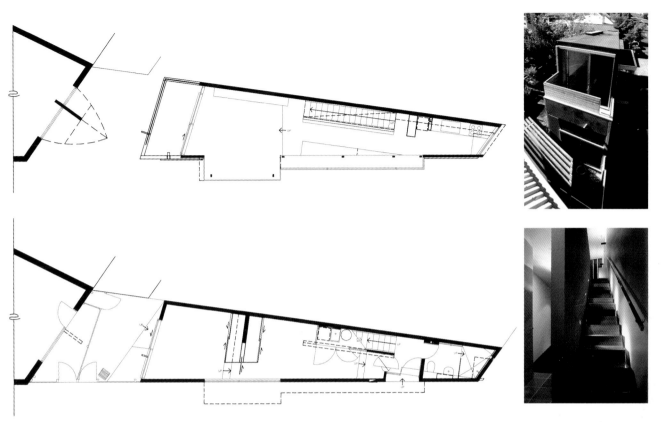

# A MODERN BOX

## HECKER PHELAN PTY LTD

Photography: Shania Shegedyn

Accepted by Paul Hecker, an interior designer, and Rob Watson, an architect, the brief was simple. 'I wanted a modern box to live in', says Hecker, who owns the small and compact house. Located behind two 1930s maisonettes, the site was originally a concrete backyard. An old shed and clothesline were the only structures. 'After subdividing the land, the only requirements were to include off-street car parking and allow for outdoor space', he says.

While the site is small, measuring approximately 11 metres by 10 metres, it is well orientated to the light and affords views over a neighbouring park. The L-shaped 'box', which features extensive glazed windows, comprises ten squares of living space spread over two levels. Unlike the traditional layout, with bedrooms upstairs and living areas below, the design was reversed. 'The main bedroom and study are downstairs and the kitchen and living area are upstairs. The high walled courtyard creates privacy', Hecker says. As a contrast to the spaces below, the living and kitchen areas are fairly exposed with views across the park.

Instead of painting the walls white to create a sense of space, Hecker chose a warm brown charcoal. 'All the colours and finishes were kept fairly uniform.

In a small space, the more finishes used, the more cluttered and confused it becomes', Hecker says. At night the interior takes on a different feel. 'The walls disappear and it feels like you're sitting in a large volume. The space can't be defined', he says.

Even though the kitchen is screened from view, it can be 'felt' from the living area. 'Some of the internal walls almost touch the perimeter walls. There's always a sense of the beyond', Hecker says. As with the limited palette of materials and colours, the furniture chosen for the home was restricted to black, brown, charcoal or white. Instead of walls becoming the feature, the lights, objects and furniture become the focus of the home. 'It is a matter of keeping things simple and creating a feeling of space', Hecker says.

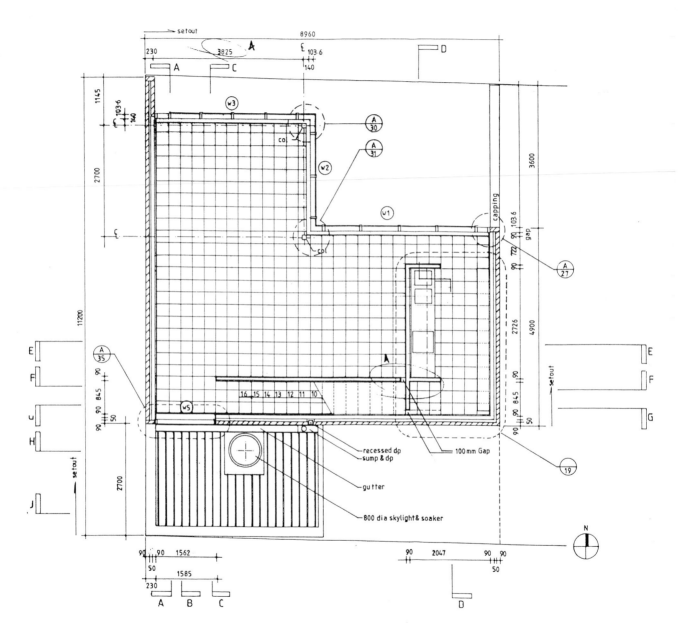

setout

8960

230    3825    103.6

140

1145

103.6
140

2700

w3

A
30

A
31

w2

3600

C

v1

capping

103.6

gap

722    90

A
27

11200

E
35

2726    4900

E

A
35

F

F

90  845  90

90  50

w5

16  15  14  13  12  11  10

90

845

90  50

G

2700

recessed dp
sump & dp

100 mm Gap

19

gutter

800 dia skylight & soaker

J

90  90    1562

50

1585

230

A    B    C

90    2047    90  90

50

D

N

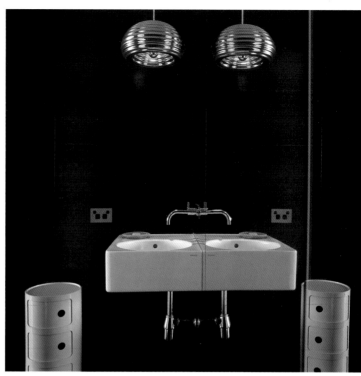

# A CLASSIC

## HOLT-DAMANT ASSOCIATES

Photography: Neil Newitt

It doesn't take long to realise who designed this classic small apartment block. Written on the blackboard attached to the back of the front door, are the words 'Frederick Romberg designed this building in 1939'.

The 24 apartments, constructed of reinforced concrete, are angled to obtain the light and a view of the garden. This apartment was recently renovated by Kathi Holt-Damant and her partner Mark, who were both attracted to the landmark building. 'These flats are extremely well planned. They take on board all the principles of good design. The breadth of the flat is orientated to the light and the concrete has a wonderful thermal mass', Holt-Damant says. A new kitchen was designed for the apartment. The wall between the kitchen and meals area was removed, which created a combined study-and-meals area.

There would not be too many small apartments where an architect would design five doors leading off one space. However, instead of a long corridor that is only used to connect spaces, Romberg's pentagonal-shaped entrance eliminates wasted space. 'Romberg was a master of planning', Holt-Damant remarks.

Given the scale of the flat, which consists of one bedroom, a combined living area, kitchen and bathroom, designing storage was important for Kathi and Mark.

A small elongated pantry next to the study only measures 250 millimetres. A unit made for the study (adjacent to the kitchen) incorporates a sliding table. 'We used German hinges to support the weight of a computer; they can take up to 60 kilos', she says. The buffet was specifically designed to conceal the television, hi-fi and video recorder. Even the glass-top buffet in the living area had to be more than a storage requirement. The many fine and intricate artefacts from Africa draw the eye into another layer of space.

As the flat is small, restraint was shown in the use of materials. The laminates, which include brushed aluminium, are an important part of the joinery. The built-in furniture reduces the amount of furniture required. Instead of several bookcases dotted around the space, one large open-grid steel bookcase was designed. As the space was tight, 'keeping it simple' and maintaining the integrity of the original design was paramount during the renovation.

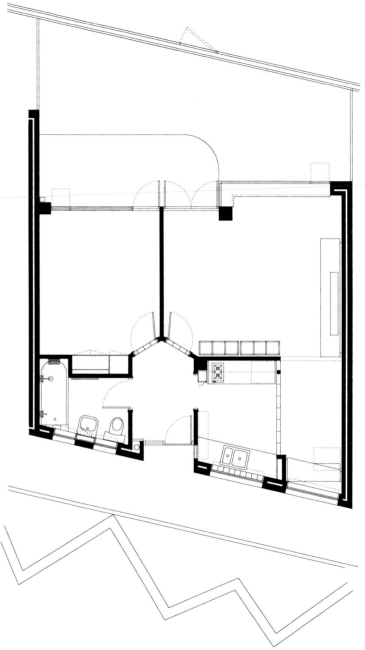

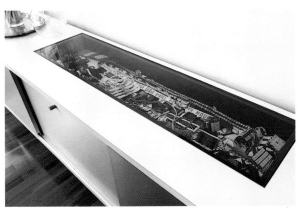

# ELEVATING THE LANEWAY

### JACKSON CLEMENTS BURROWS
### ARCHITECTS

Photography: John Gollings

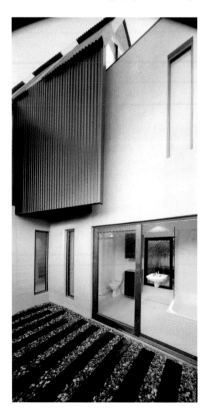

Jackson Clements Burrows Architects came across this small site in the backyard of a worker's cottage. Bordered by two- and three-storey warehouses on either side, the site measures only 5 metres by 12 metres and was not considered a realistic site to develop. Accessible only from the rear laneway, its constraints were considerable. However, instead of looking to the Victorian streetscapes in the neighbourhood for inspiration, the design was inspired by the laneway it fronts. The corrugated additions of the homes abutting the laneway and the wild overgrown gardens became a source of inspiration for the architects.

The new three-storey townhouse, built on this site, nestles into the corner of two adjoining warehouses. 'It is the only house that has an entrance to the laneway. The corrugated boundary fences are covered with vines and plants', Tim Jackson says. We wanted to design a home that looked like it had grown up against two warehouses, similar to a vine,' he says. Instead of using traditional materials such as bricks and mortar, Jackson Clements Burrows used black corrugated colour bond for the external walls, and clear polycarbonate sheeting for the windows and doors. Green panels inserted behind the polycarbonate create a green tinge to the home.

'The idea was to make the garden find its way into the building. The design could also be seen as a large, more sculptural lean-to', Jackson says.

The 12-square-metre home includes two bedrooms (one on the top floor and the other at ground level) and one large open-plan living area on the middle level. A kitchen and meals area is located at one end, with a study at the other. The spaces were designed to be flexible. While the ground-floor bedroom is orientated towards the courtyard, the bedroom on the third floor enjoys expansive views towards the city.

Jackson Clements Burrows could have dismissed the laneway environment as a collage of other people's backyards - overgrown in parts and less salubrious in others. The approach could have been to erect a brand new building that sparkled in the laneway but this remarkable new home was designed as though it were already sitting in an important streetscape.

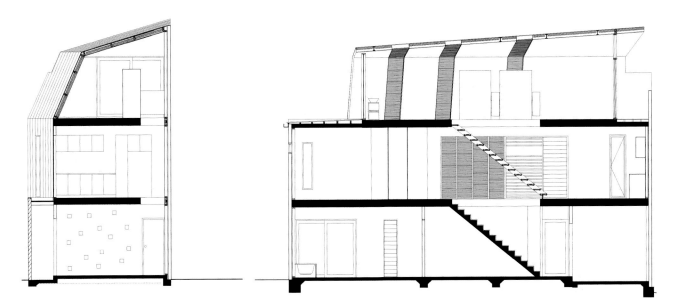

# Facing Constraints

## JAN MANTON DESIGN ARCHITECTURE

Photography: Tony Miller

When Jan Manton Design Architecture was asked to redesign this small inner-city Victorian terrace, it took into account the neighbour's concern with overlooking. 'There were a number of issues: overlooking, possible shadows and setbacks', says architect Chris Manton. 'The design really evolved as a result of the planning controls', he adds.

The house, which was closely aligned to the neighbouring backyards, also suffered from having been originally built on a sloping site (a fall of approximately 1.5 metres). 'It was almost carved into the site. The only elevation was from the home's bluestone blocks', says Manton. With a brief to design a new contemporary addition to the period home, attracting light was a large problem. 'We had to ensure privacy', he says. Light was drawn into the house via a continual skylight along the kitchen and living areas. 'It's like a shaft of light that moves between the two floors'.

As the space in the kitchen and living area was relatively small, the kitchen was treated with one large brush stroke. The white overhead cupboards in the kitchen provide the only clue as to room's function. The line of the kitchen cupboards below extends to form the joinery for the dining area. 'The one bench between the two areas is multifunctional. It was designed like a piece of furniture rather than a traditional kitchen', Manton says.

As a way of creating privacy, the new rear façade was designed with timber screens, folding out when required. The small concrete plinth, which cantilevers out from the building, defines the floor above. 'It's like a contemporary version of a Juliet balcony. It also offers some protection from the sunlight', Manton explains. The site, which only measures 6 metres wide by 16 metres in depth, had to include a new living room, a new kitchen, a laundry and powder room, together with a new main bedroom, bathroom and robe. When the list of constraints and the size of the block are put into the equation, many would not have been able to answer the brief. However, to the client's delight, the renovation went beyond their expectations, providing a light and open living environment.

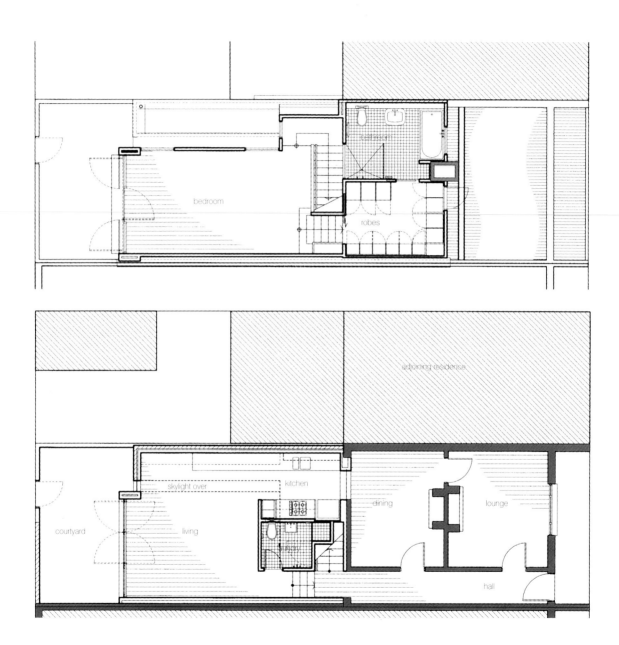

bedroom

robes

adjoining residence

skylight over

kitchen

dining

lounge

courtyard

living

hall

# Manipulating the Site

## KERSTIN THOMPSON
## ARCHITECTS

Photography: Patrick Bingham-Hall

A small narrow inner-city site is not considered an option for many families wishing to build a new home. As families extend, the general trend has been to look for larger sites in the suburbs. However, when Kerstin Thompson Architects was commissioned to design a new family home on this narrow site, the challenge was welcomed.

The house, which was designed for a five-person family, also includes space for a separate office. As Kerstin Thompson says, 'We were approached by neighbours wanting to know why we designed four bedrooms. If they wanted a family home, why didn't they look for one in the suburbs?' Rather than answer such a question, Thompson simply designed an ideal family home.

'We located the bedrooms and bathrooms downstairs which are the more private areas. We used the upstairs area for the living and kitchen areas, where there's greater light and views to the city', she says. Designing four bedrooms in such a restrictive space would have proved a challenge for most architects. Yet even with these constraints, Thompson still managed to insert a courtyard space between bedrooms. The separate office was placed above the rear garage, which affords greater privacy as a result of an internal courtyard.

The garage, which has a tilt-up glazed door, also functions as the children's play area during the day. 'The owner is on the road most of the time, so this space is ideal as an extra play area for the children'.

Instead of creating a number of predetermined spaces with one function, Thompson designed the home to be as flexible as possible. There are formal and casual areas in the home, but a series of sliding panels (designed to disappear into the wall cavities), allows for varying room sizes according to the family's requirements.

While some families head to the suburbs when their second child arrives, others are keen to remain near the city. The essence of this type of design is distilled from a desire to create flexible, adaptable spaces.

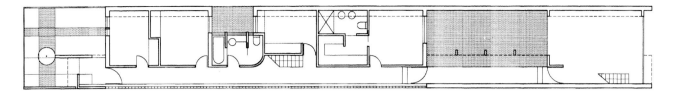

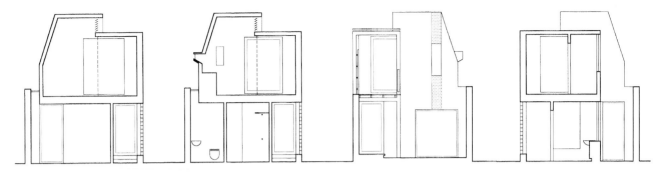

# SETTING THE STAGE
## MADDISON ARCHITECTS
Photography: Trevor Mein

With three bedrooms and a spacious living area, this 1930s townhouse is not particularly small. However, the extension of the home's original footprint by only one and a half metres makes this renovation an important story for this book.

Designed by Maddison Architects, the real story was a considerable reworking of the ground floor. The kitchen was relocated from the darkest corner of the house to the area that was previously the lounge room. A second bathroom was required and the lean-to, which was mainly used for storage, was turned into a new living area. 'You really only notice the new bay window in the living area. Opening up the ground floor was in fact quite a major exercise. We had to use enormous steel beams to carry the weight of the second floor', architect Peter Maddison says.

One of the problems Maddison faced was the dilemma of architectural styles. 'The house has a character of its own. There had to be a strong grafting of the new work which could be clearly read', Maddison says. Using steel columns and Jarrah battens laced with stainless steel wire, a 'green wall' bordering the site was designed. 'The sultana vines will soon cover the wire and create a private enclosure'.

As the kitchen was relocated to the hub of the house, small divisions were made instead of the previous solid brick wall. The central fireplace was completely removed and replaced with jarrah beams and a slatted built-in lounge. Maddison put a spin on the traditional wire meat safe, by designing a contemporary version; framed with terrazzo and lined with a perforated steel wall, the safe forms a clever extension to the breakfast bar.

The additional 1.5 metres to the living area form a stage for the owner's collection of classic post-war furniture such as Nelson, Earnes and Bertoia. When the red curtain is drawn across at night, the space takes on a more theatrical ambience. Like a stage, which is clearly defined, the floor of the new addition is delineated in terrazzo tiles in contrast to the timber floors that run through the house. 'This section is almost an invisible lightweight structure. It is referred to as one-and-a-half metres in red', Maddison says. Whether the curtain is drawn or left open, the renovation deserves the applause it receives.

# A HYBRID FORM
## MCBRIDE CHARLES RYAN
## ARCHITECTURE + INTERIOR
## DESIGN

Photography: Peter Clarke

The sound of slamming brakes is a regular disturbance for the residents who live in this building. If it is not passing automobiles making a noise, it's the continual stream of people who walk up the driveway to get a closer look. The cause of such disruption is a row of townhouses designed by McBride Charles Ryan.

For ten like-minded groups of people (among them graphic designers, architectural photographers and computer wizards), all with strong design links, it is easy to see the attraction. Instead of mapping out the site and allocating a tenth of the area for each townhouse, the development was divided into ten interlocking plates, each riding on its neighbour's back. 'They're somewhere between a traditional row house and an apartment, built in a hybrid form, as a combination of two and three storeys', says architect Rob McBride. The combination of bedrooms in a number of the townhouses was designed with flexibility in mind. A folding screen between two bedrooms can be used to separate the rooms or left open to create one larger space. In another townhouse, an open plan study can be partitioned to create a third bedroom. Like the façade, the spaces within the building carefully unfold.

The messmate façade that wraps around the communal pool and along the front fence caused whispers in design circles, however it was the dynamic, crushed reinforced-concrete exterior that proved most radical. 'We wanted to express the plastic side of concrete, something that would appear more like crushed paper or crumpled sheets, than the actual material itself', McBride says. For the firm's interior designer Debbie-Lyn Ryan, the building was partially inspired by the artistic wrappings of Christo. 'The afternoon sunlight makes the concrete appear surreal', she says. The entry to each townhouse is through a rich, jewel-like purple front door. 'It is a stained version of the marine ply that's used as a hoarding material on most building sites', says Ryan. The use of patterned stainless steel in the kitchen and polished granite on the benches and floors highlights the firm's inventiveness with materials. 'We are continually experimenting with new materials and with traditional materials in a new form'.

Instead of basement car parking and a lift taking residents to the front door, the design features a communal driveway and garden area. 'We wanted to create the feeling of a street, a place where the children can ride their bikes and residents can catch up with each other'. Unlike some apartments or townhouses, where any noise is frowned upon, the shrill sound of children's voices is appreciated in this development.

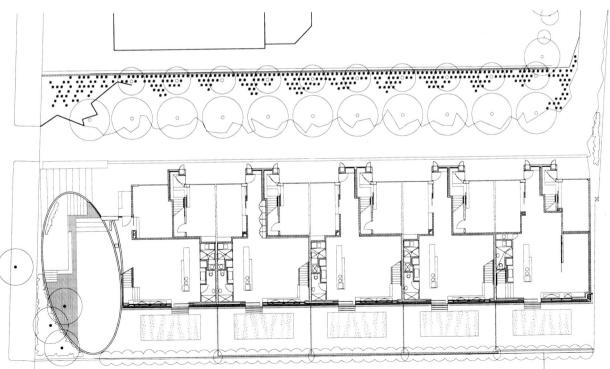

97

# FINDING A NEW MODEL

## MCGAURAN SOON ARCHITECTS

Photography: Peter Bennetts

For 31 new inner-city apartments, McGauran Soon Architects used as their model the urban village, rather than a walk-up arrangement with a shared corridor. The model was the old duplex, which was found in a number of suburbs. 'We wanted people to have their own front door, with a minimum of corridors and shared spaces', says architect Rob McGauran. Located in the centre of a busy shopping strip, the one-, two- and three-bedroom apartments are nestled behind the original façade of a hardware store. With existing townhouses on one side of the site and a substantial concrete wall on the other, 'rooms with a view' were difficult to achieve. 'We wanted to create something that would create a view and that was affordable. Su Buchanan [a former architect] came up with the stencil idea on the concrete wall. With a plywood stencil she designed an urban forest', McGauran says. Unlike a complicated trompe l'oeil, Buchanan's design is simple and contemporary. As an alternative to a series of curtains facing onto the pavement, the bedroom windows of the front units peer through the zinc roof.

To ensure that the privacy of the adjacent townhouses was not compromised, McGauran Soon extended the cedar awnings towards the boundaries.

'We really wanted to create a sense of privacy in the development. A number of the apartments have their own separate entrances. In some cases, one staircase leads to two apartments', McGauran says. There were a number of options given for the finishes of the apartments. 'We gave a few alternatives. One option for an interior was darker and moodier. Another was lighter and more neutral'. Even though the apartments are relatively small, from 55–95 square metres, the generous terraces increase the feeling of space.

As McGauran says, 'We concentrated on the quality of the project and ensured that the spaces were flexible. We wanted to design something that we would want to live in, irrespective of whether it was a house or an apartment'.

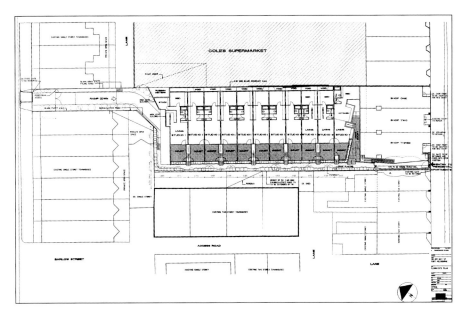

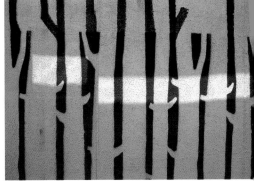

# MULTIFACETED
## MUTIPLICITY

Photography: Andreas Schmidt & Shania Shegedyn

For architect Tim O'Sullivan and his partner Sioux Clark, an interior designer, the renovation of this small warehouse has been a continuous project over the last three years. As Clark says, 'Since it was designed for our own home, we tended to put it on the back burner after our work commitments'. The warehouse, which was originally used by a shirt manufacturer, was subdivided by Multiplicity soon after its purchase. 'We thought that we would sell off the smaller of the two spaces and use the one that fronts the main road as our home and office combined', says O'Sullivan. However, after numerous inspections by less than visionary developers, the 'For Sale' advertisement was removed and Tim and Sioux decided to develop the smaller space themselves.

The warehouse was essentially a shell when Multiplicity moved in. Even the concrete floors were defective. Instead of lamenting the loss of a polished concrete floor, the two renovators used tongue-and-groove plywood flooring for both the floors and the walls. O'Sullivan took the time to lay pebbles in the kitchen and bathroom himself, in a pattern that resembled a riverbed. 'In many warehouse renovations, a small courtyard is wedged into the space and never used. The idea of the pebbles was to give the impression of a sheltered riverbed that would have a sense of the outdoors', says O'Sullivan.

One of the ways Multiplicity defined the space, without enclosing it, was to change levels between the areas. The 'thermoclear' plastic-studded walls that act as the central spine in the warehouse also create a sense of transparency, as does the recycled 1960s mesh screen that encloses the staircase to the two bedrooms above. One of the hallmarks of this firm is integrating materials from the past, while still providing a sharp and contemporary look. 'The stainless steel sink had to be specifically made for the kitchen. We were luckier with the bath (circa 1940s), which came from a farmhouse', Clark says. As the kitchen is open to the living areas, the utilitarian aspects of the kitchen (the fridge and the microwave) were relegated to the pantry area. While the treatment in most kitchens is often uniform, Multiplicity used a subtle range of colours and materials in their design.

The lounge area, which is defined by a change in level, also has a full view of the bathroom, though the toilet area has a door. Given the sheer artistry of the bathroom, with its floating steel bath and pebbled flooring, its open plan is appreciated. The warehouse, which is reminiscent of a sepia photograph, is a welcome surprise in the laneway.

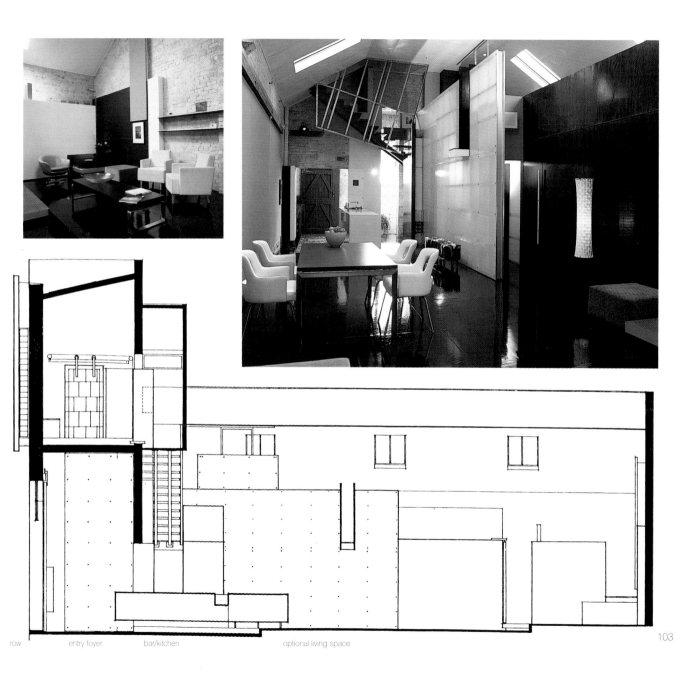

row      entry foyer      bar/kitchen      optional living space

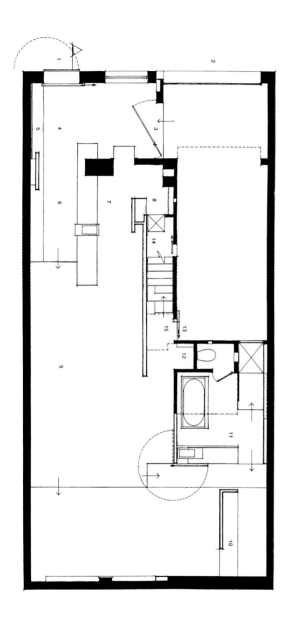

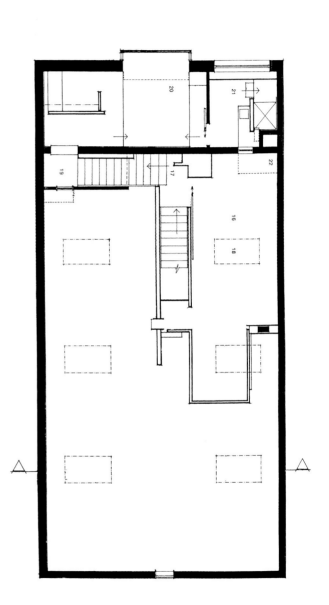

# BLURRING THE BOUNDARIES

## NEIL & IDLE ARCHITECTS

Photography: Trevor Mein

For architects, the building they work in is often as important as the homes they design. For the architectural firm Neil & Idle, this new building has provided a sense of identity for their practice and a clever and comfortable retreat.

The corner site was small to start with, measuring only 205 square metres. However, the site was further sub-divided to build a separate photographic studio. For architect Chris Idle, whose father owns a plastic factory, the material for the new building was never an issue. 'I've always been interested in plastic', says Idle. The polycarbonate double-layered skin that was selected for the building would not only give the building a sense of depth, but would also create a sense of privacy and diffuse the light in the process. From the curved polycarbonate extrusion on the street façade, to creating a layered and tactile composition at the front, the plastic appears to literally weave in and out of the building. In contrast to the plastic, a marine ply feature wall highlights the positive and negative play of organic shapes.

The office occupies the ground level and the mezzanine above. Tucked away behind a door on the mezzanine level, a staircase leads to the conference area. 'For more casual meetings we tend to use the lounge and deck area.

If we are discussing plans, we will use the dining area', Idle says. The lounge area, which could double as the 'cone of silence' (think *Get Smart*), appears to change in form. Blurred silos in a neighbouring street become high-rise buildings, with the polycarbonate being activated by the moving taillights from passing cars.

The kitchen was simply devised to cater for work functions. The stainless steel bench top takes an unexpected turn and becomes storage for trays and kitchen appliances. In a similarly deceptive way, the kitchen's splashback takes on the appearance of additional cupboards. 'It's simply sprayed MDF board', Cameron Neil says.

Drivers get out of their cars to touch the building. Others walk by with strained expressions. 'I think that some people don't find the building serious enough!', laughs Neil.

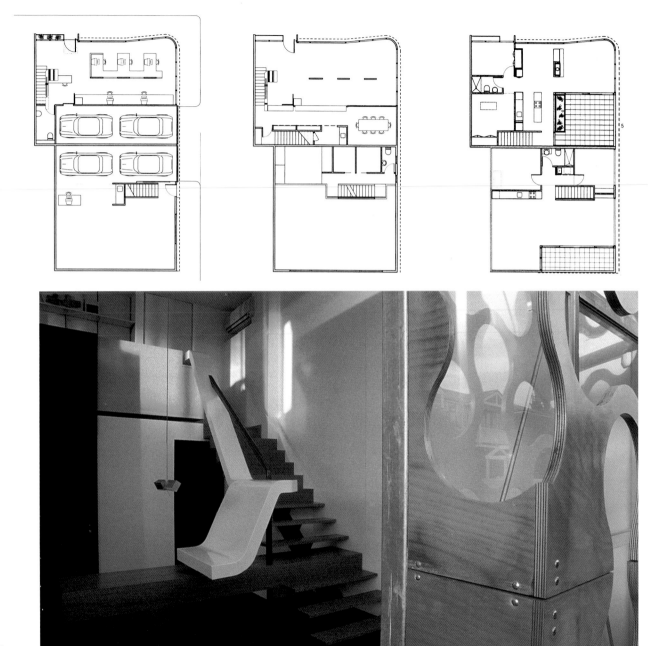

# A Small Footprint

## NEOMETRO ARCHITECTS

Photography: Peter Clarke & Trevor Mein

A site measuring only 14 metres by 9 metres would not tempt many people into building a new home for themselves, let alone a number of apartments. However, for Neometro Architects, known for their clever manipulation of space, the size of the site did not deter their plans.

Located down a laneway, the site is situated behind an auto repair shop. Marked out for five car parking spaces, it was the air space above that attracted the team to develop the site. With a 19-metre-high wall on the north side of the lane (containing a wine bar, apartments and studio), the lane is also a busy thoroughfare. Out of the five car spaces and the air space above, Neometro Architects created four dwellings that could be used for both living and working in. 'It was designed with flexibility in mind. It might suit a one-person operation such as a jeweller, who also sleeps on the mezzanine above', architect Clare McAllister of Neometro Architects says.

With only 11 squares of space to work in, the dwellings resemble mini-lofts. 'We see these spaces as containers for living. They were designed to create a more affordable form of infill housing', McAllister says. One of the options in designing the spaces could have been to construct a protective box, creating an inward view.

However, in contrast, Neometro Architects included north-facing double-height glazed windows that face onto the lane. 'People deal with privacy in their own ways. Curtains can be put up in the living areas and the sleeping mezzanines can be further enclosed with timber screenings', she says. However, an alternative strategy of infill glazed facades was adopted, acting like wide-angle lenses to draw as much light as possible into the interior of each unit.

In order to maximise the useable floor area, many of the services, including the stairwell, were designed at the rear of the container. 'A standard 11-square flat built in the 1970s would feel a lot smaller', McAllister says. To find four of the five car spaces remaining on the site is also a remarkable feat. Only the fifth car space has been sacrificed for the central staircase and entry. As the laneway is typically narrow, the apartments on the first floor were set back at an angle to allow for the motorist's vision. However, on the top floor the corner apartment cantilevers into the airspace. A small footprint marks a skilful design.

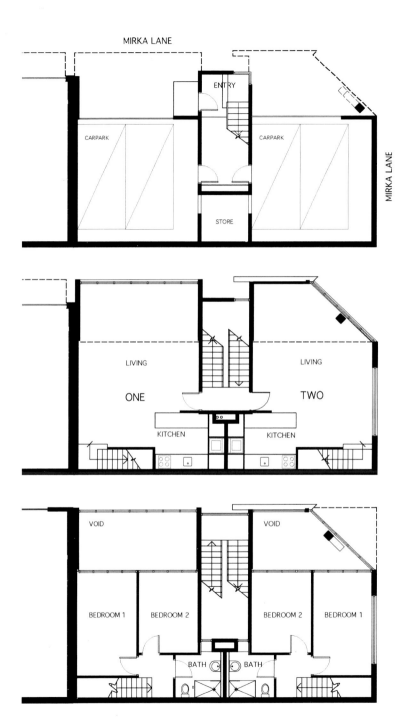

MIRKA LANE

ENTRY

CARPARK

CARPARK

MIRKA LANE

STORE

LIVING

ONE

TWO

LIVING

KITCHEN

KITCHEN

VOID

VOID

BEDROOM 1

BEDROOM 2

BEDROOM 2

BEDROOM 1

BATH

BATH

# A New
# Direction
## NICHOLAS GIOIA ASSOCIATES
Photography: Trevor Mein

A small house does not have to feel enclosed. Even a house less than ten squares in size can take on larger proportions. For architect Nicholas Gioia, creating a number of views was also important.

With most small terrace homes taking in at best one view (a small rear garden), finding new angles to enhance the exterior can be difficult. However, Gioia was able to insert a small slither of a courtyard between the bedrooms and the living area at the rear. Although miniscule, the courtyard acts as a light well for the main bedroom and the kitchen. 'The sunlight from the courtyard activates the spaces', says Gioia. 'Where a courtyard could not be inserted onto the site [three courtyards were included], the sunlight is able to penetrate through the protected glazing and concealed skylights. The awning across the rear façade filters the light during the warmer months', he adds.

The design called for 'restraint, precision and simplicity'. As the space is small, the design called for a minimal and efficient use of joinery. As a way of creating the feeling of space in the new living area, a low-lying built-in cabinet (including the fireplace and flue) was designed as the main focus. In the small compact bathroom an unadorned, simple timber vanity is accompanied by a singular floating shelf.

As a means of enriching the space, the division between the kitchen and living areas is achieved with floating cabinets in timber and laminates. The cabinets, which are internally illuminated, create another dimension to the spaces. The joinery clearly defines the spaces and also acts as clever visual devices in the house. The transparency extends to the perforated feature wall at the end of the passage.

While most small terraces feature a shotgun corridor down one side and one restricted view to a rear courtyard, this home includes a number of fine angles and captivating views. At night, the graphic lines of the home continue to activate the senses. The vertical beams of the awning appear to extend indefinitely. As Gioia says, 'The house originally felt hemmed in. There weren't many directions in which you could go'. Today, exploring only the one path is no longer an option.

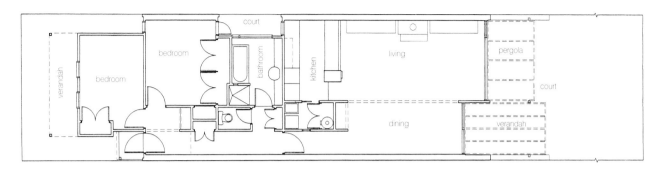

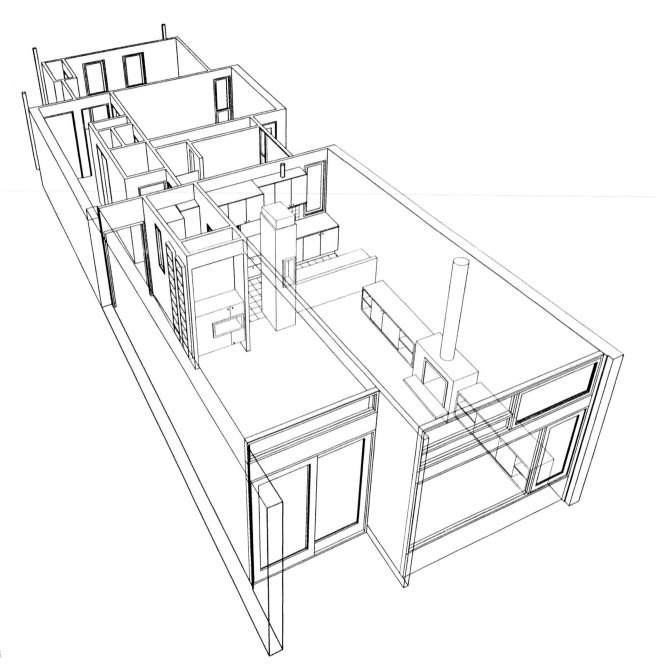

# DESIGNED FOR LIVING NOT FOR SALE

### INTERIOR DESIGN: ANDREW PARR, SJB INTERIOR DESIGN

Photography: James Grant

Interior designer Andrew Parr ignored the advice of real estate agents when it came to designing his new home. Located on a small site, 7 metres wide by 17 metres in depth, the new concrete and steel home was not about fitting in as many rooms as possible. 'It probably won't read well on real estate brochures', says Parr, a director of SJB Interior Design.

The house consists of one continuous open plan kitchen and living area on the ground floor, bordered by two protected courtyard areas. Upstairs, there are two bedrooms, with the main bedroom partially open to the living area below. Even the ensuite, which is normally tucked away, forms part of the bedroom, its glass wall and venetian blinds controlling the privacy. In the same way, the vanity basin is part of the bedroom furniture. As Parr says, 'Most shower recesses are so depressing, with no relation to the outside', he says. 'There is nothing better than being able to look out at the sky and see what is going on'.

Like the main bedroom, which is not compartmentalised, walls don't segment the kitchen and living areas below. 'This house does not have a starting and a finishing point.

There is a fluidity that you lack when you compartmentalise space. This is more a building with transition zones', Parr says. The neutral palette of materials - black marble for the kitchen, black steel beams for the staircase and black lacquered timber for the treads and on the floor above - create a simple and graphic composition in the space. The only enclosure to the staircase is a sharp steel handrail. 'I have designed as few intrusions into the space as possible. When you are working with small spaces, it is important to keep things simple'.

While the generous void over the living area could have been designed as another room (and satisfied real estate agents), for Parr, who lives in the house, the extra room probably wouldn't have been used and the living room less visited and enjoyed. Instead light streams into the living and bedrooms and there is no feeling of being hemmed in. With courtyards on either side of the house, the feeling is more like being in a freestanding villa than a small inner-city townhouse.

# DESIGNING A NEW LAYER

## SHELLEY PENN

Photography: Trevor Mein

Gritty, raw and honest - these are words that come to mind on inspecting this small, renovated warehouse. Flanked by Victorian cottages, the external red brick walls are covered with layers of graffiti that helped to steer the renovation. The owner, a graphic designer and painter, didn't want to live in a warehouse that had been glossed over.

The original brickwork, pine floors and timber trusses were intact, however the orientation to the sunlight only included one original timber door on the second floor. 'Even though the space was sufficient for my client's requirements, it was fairly dark', says architect Shelley Penn, who designed the renovation.

With respect for the past, the brief to Penn was to reveal, rather than sandblast, the walls. 'It was originally used as a vinegar factory. I wanted to retain its tough exterior, with the new work clearly read from its past', Penn says. Only subtle changes were made to the ground floor, which included the retention of the worn ceiling rafters. The main structural change was to insert a galvanised steel box on the eastern façade, which contains a new bathroom and bedroom. The east-west light and ventilation was manipulated by slightly elevating the steeply pitched roof.

The ground floor was left relatively intact, and a kitchen was built on the floor above. New hoop pine ply cupboards were framed by a 'mild steel' brace. The bedroom, which lies at the top of the stairs, is nestled into its new steel wing. Set back from the building's façade, the new bedroom is given breathing space by the insertion of a small outdoor deck. Mindful of circulation, Penn incorporated louvred glass panes in the bedroom walls. The heavy timber door, which blocked the light, was replaced with glass.

The brief was simple: one bedroom, a bathroom, a kitchen/living area and studio. But the design issues were far more complex. Plastering the rough walls and removing the graffiti would have transformed the home into a pristine showpiece, but its history and integrity would have been lost in the process.

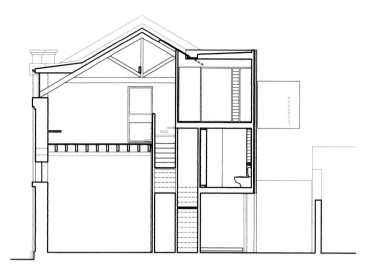

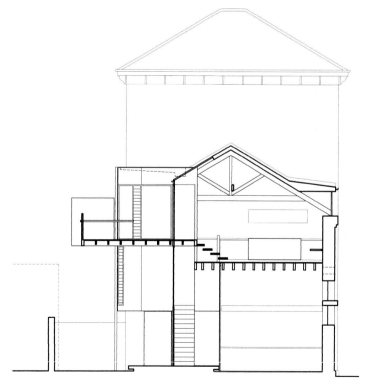

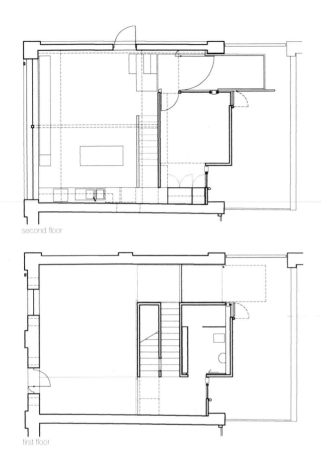

second floor

first floor

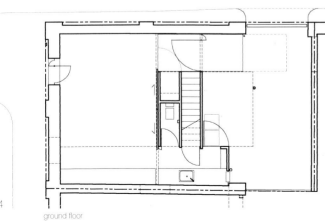

ground floor

124

# PUSHING THE BOUNDARIES

## PROVAN BURDETT ARCHITECTS
Photography: Peter Clarke

A few metres can make all the difference when you are renovating a single-fronted Victorian terrace. This home benefited from a site that dog-legged to a side boundary.

The original home consisted of two bedrooms, a central bathroom, and the kitchen and living area at the rear. 'The house was quite dark. The kitchen had been renovated in the early seventies, but it was looking fairly tired', says architect Tania Provan, who renovated the house with architect David Burdett. 'The rear courtyard wasn't used. It was overgrown with bamboo', she says. The client's brief was for a sense of space and a functional courtyard area. Provan Burdett Architects allocated the overgrown courtyard area for the new kitchen. The remainder of the building's footprint was kept intact. As the boundary wall was stepped, some of the more inaccessible spaces were included in areas that couldn't be seen, such as storage and pantry areas for the kitchen.

To improve upon the solid door to the rear courtyard, and only two traditional windows to the side courtyard, Provan and Burdett designed full-length glass doors to frame the living room. As the client wanted to work in a more light-filled space, a workstation made of jarrah and painted custom wood was accommodated into the new kitchen.

The computer can be stored below, should additional bench space for food preparation be required. With space being a luxury, Provan Burdett included room for wine storage in the kitchen. 'The wine is concealed in the kickboard under the kitchen cupboards', Provan says.

The client had lived in Asia for a considerable time, and the brief included a shelving unit to accommodate the many artefacts collected. 'We designed a shelving system that could be used for books or objects. It acts as a focal point in the living area', Provan says. Unlike some clients who come to an architect with a wish list in one hand and magazine clippings in the other, the owner of this home was keen to benefit from the architect's skills. 'There were no preconceptions. She was interested in what an architect could deliver'. For a site that measures only five metres at some points, the feeling within is surprisingly spacious.

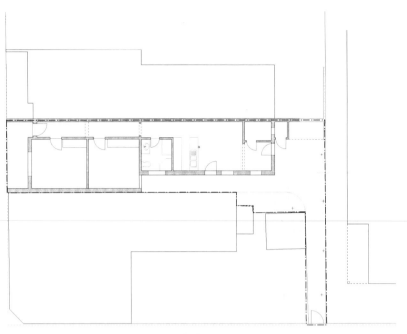

OSBORNE STREET

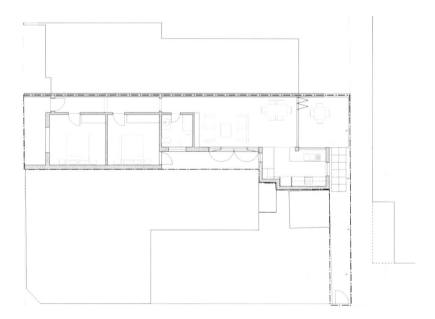

# LET THERE BE LIGHT

## MICHAEL RAHILL

Photography: Robert Colvin & Michael Rahill

This small ground-floor apartment was dark and oppressive, despite the fact it was designed to catch the sunlight. The 1930s apartment, of approximately 73 square metres, suffered from everything being in the wrong place. 'The area that received the most light was wasted by being occupied by the kitchen and bathroom, with both rooms having small windows', says architect Michael Rahill, who was given the brief to redesign the apartment. Where the light was needed, in the living areas, there was only an unimpressive view to a stairwell leading to a neighbouring apartment.

Rahill completely rearranged the apartment's layout. 'I presented my clients with a number of options. They ended up selecting the most adventurous option', Rahill says. The area that was previously the bathroom became the kitchen and the former kitchen became part of the new enlarged living area. One of the major concerns was bringing in light to the living spaces. The steel-cased 1930s framed windows were relatively ineffective in drawing the light into the space. New large windows were installed in the new living room's wall. To create privacy (the apartment abuts a communal pathway) white glass was used. 'It glows when the sun shines upon it. At most times of the day the room is flooded with a soft calm light', Rahill says.

In the main bedroom, bringing in the light was also a priority. 'I designed a new highlight window between the robes and the ceiling. It means that light can also find its way into the bathroom', he says.

When it came to redesigning the kitchen, it was important to keep the space as light as possible. The only delineation from the living areas comes in the form of a small fin wall inserted between the spaces. The kitchen is still quite small, but it was designed to be efficient. Appliances are concealed and materials are kept simple. The blue-green laminate is one of the few colours used in the apartment. While the apartment is relatively small, it feels considerably larger. The additional light amplifies the space, not only through the enlarged windows, but also through the enlarged doorways. All the doors and internal openings were taken up to the ceiling. The space flows from one room to the next, creating a more unified and larger apartment in the process.

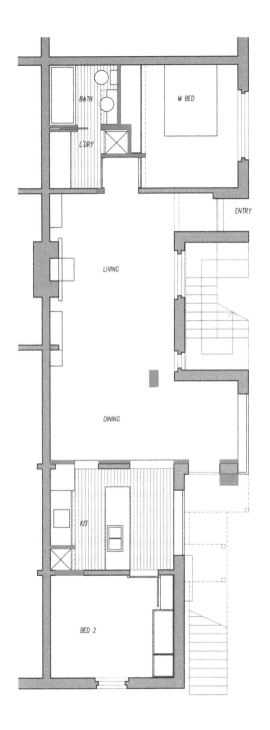

BATH

L'DRY

M BED

ENTRY

LIVING

DINING

KIT

BED 2

# A VISION
## CRAIG ROSSETTI
Photography: Andrew Ashton

When architect Craig Rossetti could not convince developers to build his townhouses, he set about convincing friends to share his vision. With the location being in an industrial suburb that is quickly becoming one of the city's more desirable addresses, it wasn't difficult finding partners interested in the venture. 'I hired a crane and bought a few bottles of champagne. When they saw the views that would eventually be available from the townhouses, most friends signed up', says Rossetti.

The site, which was vacant, originally contained three worker's cottages. With six three-storey townhouses planned for the site, the width for each townhouse was just under four metres. The ground floor consists of the living area and kitchen, the second level contains the two bedrooms, and there is a study and roof deck on the third level. With spectacular city views from the roof terrace, it is understandable that corks were popping on the day they took possession. To overcome the narrow dimensions within, Rossetti left the concrete block walls exposed. The concrete blocks were simply sandblasted and banded with charcoal skirtings. 'Using plaster would have added 140 millimetres and would have increased the cost', he says.

As a way of increasing the sense of space, Rossetti took 300 millimetres off the height of the ceiling in the middle level and gave it to the ground level. 'The three-metre ceiling heights are more important in the living areas. I also used up-lights on the walls to accentuate the height. I didn't want pools of light on the floor'.

The brushed metal screen that divides the living area from the kitchen replaces traditional walls and offers glimpses between the spaces. The open staircase, which winds up the three levels, was also designed to take in slithers of views and to allow for ventilation throughout the levels. 'I designed two ponds in the front and rear courtyard. The winds bring the cooler air from the ponds through the low windows at both ends. Ventilation is crucial in small spaces', Rossetti says.

As Rossetti says, 'When you have a limited amount of space, it is better to design a simple large element than includes several smaller ideas. You don't want to feel hemmed in'. As friends gather on the roof terrace for drinks, they can see numerous townhouses now in the process of development.

# A FUTURE SHACK

## SEAN GODSELL ARCHITECTS

Photography: Earl Carter

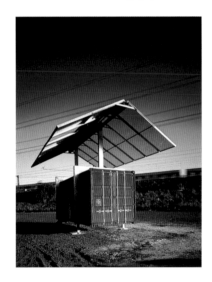

This small shack, presently located on an industrial site, doesn't have the traditional features of a small house. Instead of windows and a front porch, architect Sean Godsell's small shack is built within a recycled shipping container. The only visible addition to the form is a parasol-like roof that hovers above (for sun protection) and four adjustable steel legs that protrude from the base. 'These legs allow you to erect the homes on a variety of terrain at short notice. You don't have to prepare the site, which is a considerable cost saver', Godsell says. 'I was thinking of the need to provide short- to mid-term relief for countries that were in crisis, after a war or a flood', he says. As a means of selling the idea, Godsell built the prototype model.

The container, which is made of Cor-Ten steel, is normally painted for the shipping industry. However, Godsell leaves the container unpainted so that the Cor-Ten's orange patina can weather with the elements. Approximately two squares in space, the shack could be accommodated on someone's back veranda. However, within the confines of the container, Godsell cleverly illustrates the importance of design. Two beds are concealed within the insulated walls and change the living room into a bedroom at night. The kitchen table,

concealed in the opposing wall, makes an appearance first thing in the morning and can be packed away during the day.

Those looking for the service areas within a home, like the kitchen and bathroom, need only open the bank of craft wood cupboards to find the sink and place for the refrigerator. With a house of this size, finding a bathroom in any form comes as a surprise. However, instead of a makeshift toilet/washing area, opening a door reveals a finely executed bathroom, lined with marine ply and containing stainless steel accessories. 'I wanted to design something that was durable and robust, but also had a certain level of comfort. The walls for example are insulated. I also wanted to make sure that the kitchen area was light [two skylights were inserted into the crate]', Godsell says.

The shack might not have a separate meals area and there is only one bedroom, although technically it could be referred to as having an ensuite. However, given the limitations and the size of the budget, the interior is both finely crafted and ingeniously resolved. Godsell's small shack not only speaks the universal language of shelter, but it is a reminder of the important role that architecture plays in finding solutions for human dilemmas.

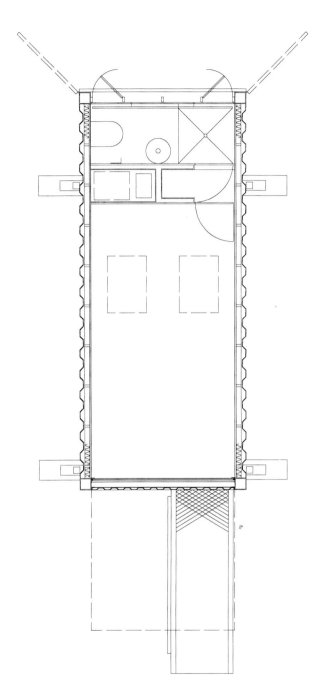

# A NARROW TUBE
## SIX DEGREES ARCHITECTS
Photography: Trevor Mein

Measuring only 10 metres by 36 metres, this site was originally a brick factory. In the inner city, where space is at a premium, four townhouses were designed in what would be a single-dwelling site in the suburbs.

Designed by Six Degrees Architects, one of the townhouses is now home to one of the directors, architect James Legge. Legge's home, which shares the street with another of the townhouses, is approximately five metres in width. Designed over three levels, the home consists of a garage on the ground floor, kitchen and living areas on the first floor and two bedrooms above. 'It is essentially a tube. The details create a significant part of the architecture', says Legge. 'Most of the formal expression is directed towards the two elevations, the rear and the front', he adds. The front elevation to the street was designed with new and reclaimed leadlight. Steel pergolas adorning the façade will soon be covered with wisteria and jasmine. 'I wanted to explore the idea of a façade that changes over the year with the seasons. It will never look static'.

As the townhouse is narrow, the interior walls (at the perimeter) were rendered instead of plastered. 'You try and gain a few millimetres where ever possible. The staircases are also fairly narrow, 800 mm to the first floor and 700 mm to the second', Legge explains.

The townhouse also features built-in joinery to compensate for the width of the home. The joinery at the top of the stairs acts as a bookshelf and sideboard for the dining room. 'It is part of the balustrade. The dining room table is also built in. There is a series of linear elements in the space. The furniture divides the spaces', he says. As a way of creating a possible third bedroom on the first floor, the cupboards in the study area can be drawn out to form an entirely contained room. 'The cupboard wall is on wheels. It gives you the option of creating an additional room if guests stay over'.

The powder room is tucked behind a yellow feature wall and the stairs to the bedrooms above are concealed behind the living room wall. 'It is a matter of creating a few surprises. Most people think that you can't define and control small spaces. You really need to carefully define and work with what you have. In many ways, small spaces can end up richer than larger projects'.

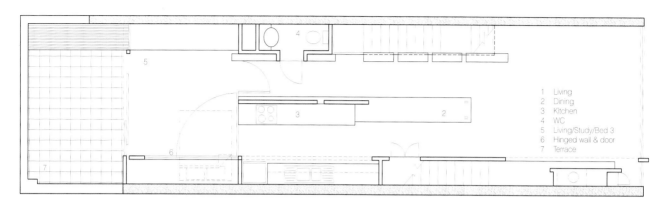

1 Living
2 Dining
3 Kitchen
4 WC
5 Living/Study/Bed 3
6 Hinged wall & door
7 Terrace

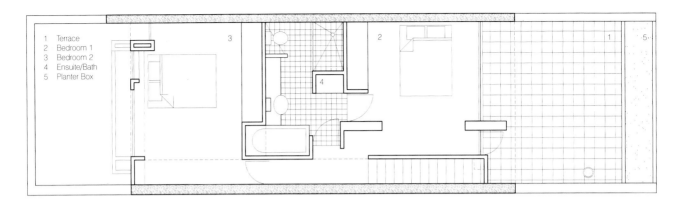

1 Terrace
2 Bedroom 1
3 Bedroom 2
4 Ensuite/Bath
5 Planter Box

# A SENSE OF SPACE

## SJB ARCHITECTS

Photography: Trevor Mein & Tim Griffith

Located on the city fringe, this building was previously a multi-storey office block before being converted into apartments. For the owners, Thais Clark and architect Alfred de Bruyne, a director of SJB Architects, their space in the building was part of the office caféteria.

While this space was relatively generous compared to other apartments, approximately 15 squares, it required considerable reworking to be made a home. 'One of the problems with the space was the major column in what was to be the living and dining area. It cut up the space', de Bruyne says. As a way of concealing the column, which is a structural support, a study nook was designed around the structure. Elevated, the new study area creates another layer to the space. 'The joinery enclosing the study doubles as storage and conceals the sound system and the television', he says. With the inclusion of a study, the dining and living area is defined in an L-shape rather than left open. 'The study forms a screen but you can still see past the form', he adds.

The sense of space starts at the front door. Upon entering, it is easy to appreciate the dimensions of the apartment. From the front door to the alcove between the two bedrooms, the length is at least 10 metres. 'The long vista reinforces the space. We also placed several planter boxes on the terrace, on the diagonal. It draws your eye to the edges of the terrace and creates a space and volume', explains de Bryune. Andrew Parr, an interior designer and director of SJB Interior Design, collaborated with the couple on the project. 'We have worked together for years. Andrew knew what we were trying to achieve', he adds.

The kitchen, which is graphically outlined in an alcove, was designed to conceal appliances. When it comes to creating a sense of space, even the finishes require careful selection. 'There are lots of reflective surfaces on the joinery. We used two-pack paint finishes on the cupboards to catch the light. It adds a level of reflectivity to the space and creates a sense of depth in the process', de Bryune says.

While it would not be hard to find a suburban house of this size, finding one that feels as spacious may prove difficult. The apartment is light-filled, features high ceilings, and appears endless. As de Bryune says, 'With smaller spaces, you need to be able to look beyond a point'.

main bedroom

study

second bedroom

study

# A COMPLETE MAKEOVER

## STANIC HARDING
## ARCHITECTURE + INTERIORS
Photography: Paul Gosney

This three-storey townhouse was originally built in the 1980s. However, after nearly 20 years, it wasn't just the size of the house, but the layout that needed a complete makeover. The architects Stanic Harding stripped all three levels, designed a completely new rear façade and drew the courtyards into the interior space. The new pond on the ground level became the main focus from all levels.

The rooms were also redesigned by the architects. The lower level is now a garage, TV/guestroom and courtyard, the middle level is the kitchen, dining and living area, while the top level is the bedroom and study. 'The house is small, so all the elements are carefully proportioned and placed. A number of major elements float and slip above the ground plane to extend the spaces', says architect Andrew Stanic. With ventilation being a crucial factor in designing small spaces, the architects created a 'slice' across each level to allow light and air to penetrate and circulate within the home. Finely crafted aluminium-slatted floor bridges slice the flooring at each level and help to define either a change in level or function. Open stairs, slatted floors, glass, considered openings, frames and worked edges assist in enriching these vistas.

The ornamental pond with a 'floating' pebble-clad screen was designed as the focus of the exterior space. Audible on all three levels from within the house the sound of water can even be heard from the louvred main bedroom on the top floor. As Stanic says, 'Due to the long and narrow floor plan, the elements within the space had to be carefully arranged to allow for an uninterrupted physical and visual connection to the house and its courtyard. It was important to reinforce the vistas as it is essentially a small house'.

Unlike many narrow three-storey homes, where each level is clearly segmented from the other, this home appears as one continuous and fluid design. Common elements connect each level and the sound of water throughout the house is as fluid as the design itself.

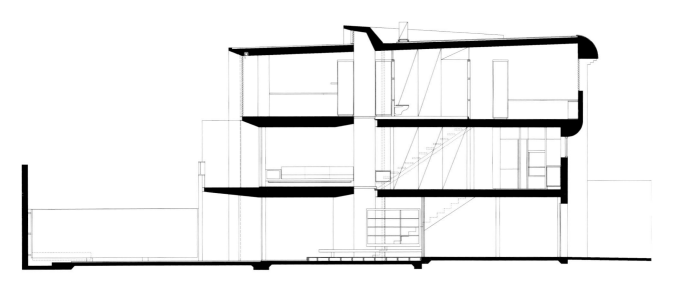

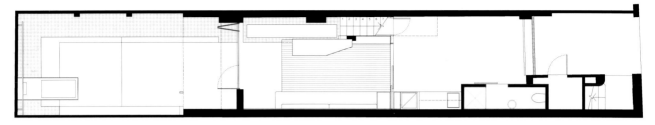

# PERFORMING GYMNASTICS

## STEPHEN VARADY
## ARCHITECTURE

Photography: Stephen Varady

This 40-square-metre apartment had a view to rely on, but little else. Even with the views, the white walls and a polished floor would not be enough to transform this home into a spacious abode. For architect Stephen Varady, the design called for a more inventive approach.

While white walls and polished floorboards feature in the design, the approach is far more complex. 'The approach treats the interior as a series of intersecting, white triangular prisms. It was about exploring the sculptural possibilities of forms when they are tied to specific functional constraints', Varady says. Instead of a blank white laminate veneer for the kitchen cupboards, Varady's are finely layered in depth. As intriguing as a piece of sculpture, the kitchen cupboards invite a tactile response. 'The intent was to hide what was not necessary, bringing it to life only when required. Elements fold down, slide out or open when the occasion calls for', he says.

The dining table, which forms a bridge between the kitchen and lounge area, also disappears into a wall when not in use. Only the fixed 'floating' canopy above the dining area is a continual reminder that there is always room for dinner guests. The same clever detail was applied to the installation of the television set. In most homes, the television set is fixed permanently to a corner of the living room.

However, in this apartment the suspended television glides along a track on the ceiling. 'It can be viewed from any point in the apartment, or folded up like a piece of furniture or sculpture in the corner', he says.

While the main bedroom can be screened from the living areas, it can remain open to give the apartment a more spacious feel. When the sliding doors are closed, the entrance to the bedroom cleverly resembles one of the many kitchen cupboards, only on a different scale. While many designers would have relied on the views to create a sense of space, Varady ingeniously manipulates and crafts the spaces from within, making the views almost secondary in the process. When certain views couldn't be achieved in the space, Varady brought in the use of mirrors. 'When mirrors are strategically placed, the apartment reads as more than it is. The large mirror next to the main northern window creates a much wider vista'.

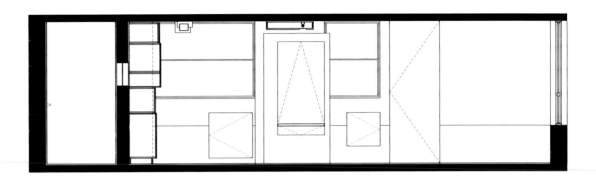

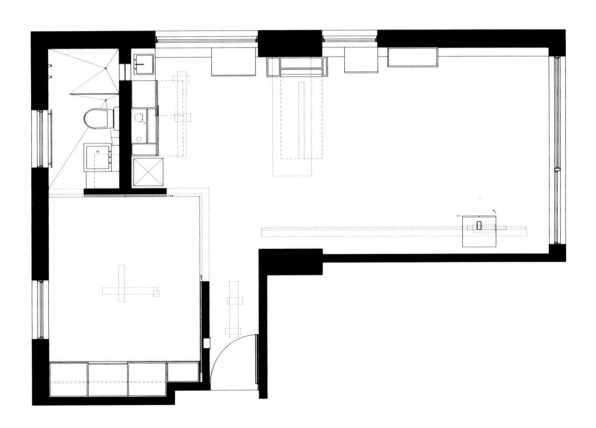

# A Worker's
# Cottage
## SWANEY DRAPER ARCHITECTS
Photography: Peter Hyatt

In a row of three, this small worker's cottage occupies an equally small site (4 metres by 18 metres). Derelict and consisting of only two rooms and a small addition, it is not surprising that there was very little interest in purchasing the property.

However, architect Sally Draper of Swaney Draper Architects could appreciate the few redeeming features of the cottage. Its location for one, in the inner city, was sufficient to warrant further action. 'It was almost uninhabitable. There were basically only two rooms and a small lean-to for the bathroom. You literally had to stand in sideways to even use the kitchen. The front door opened directly onto the lounge room', Draper says.

In the front room, a nib wall was created to ensure a sense of arrival rather than a sense of intrusion. The room was then converted into a study, together with a separate bathroom. However, when it came to redesigning the rear of the home, more drastic measures were called for. 'We designed the rear extension with the same profile as the façade of the cottage and designed a continuous band of louvred glass windows. When you are working with small spaces, ventilation and light are crucial', Draper says. As a way of increasing the floor space, a new mezzanine was inserted into the new one-and-a-half-storey volume.

Open to the living area below, the bedroom feels considerably larger than the size of the double bed. 'The mezzanine was designed away from the wall to allow for circulation. It creates a breathing space', she says.

When it comes to working with small spaces, Draper's advice is to use a limited palette of materials and to ensure that functions overlap. 'There is really only the timber, the concrete slab floor and the white walls. When it came to functional requirements, such as storage areas, one unit had to be multi-functional. The bookcase had to include the books, the television unit and things that couldn't be accommodated on the floor. The whole house is only about 50 square metres'.

Given the size of the cottage, even a staircase could not be accommodated. Instead, a timber ladder to the mezzanine bedroom was used. The cottage remains two rooms deep and the façade is still relatively intact. However, Swaney Draper's design clearly explores not only the possibilities within a small space, but the richness that can be achieved from a simple worker's cottage.

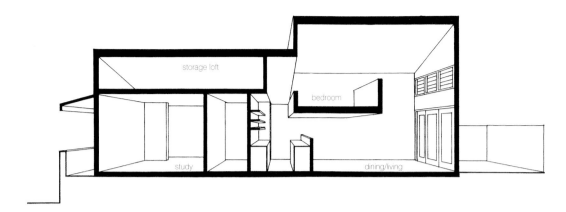

storage loft

bedroom

study

dining/living

# CREATING A VOID
## TONKIN ZULAIKHA GREER ARCHITECTS
Photography: Patrick Bingham-Hall

The dramatic voids created in this apartment compensate for the size. The apartment building, designed by Tonkin Zulaikha Greer Architects contains six one- and two-bedroom apartments. In the two-bedroom apartments (pictured) the large internal gesture of the void deflects from the limited floor space. As mentioned by the architects: 'the bedrooms to the north were unable to have northern windows because of their proximity to the site boundary. They were therefore orientated to the internal void'.

The two-storey glass wall that leads on to the deck gives the apartment a feeling of space, far greater than the 90 square metres provided. While the void enlarges the space, the balcony lines above draw one's eye to the external views. Given the apartment's exposure to the elements, the architects were keen to screen the direct sunlight, particularly during the warmer months. A large retractable screen ensures both sunlight and privacy can be modulated.

The staircase was also designed to create a feeling of space. Instead of enclosing the treads with a blank wall, Tonkin Zulaikha Greer used stainless steel wire. While this detail doesn't create additional floor space, it certainly extends the width of the apartment. The steel bridge above, which acts as a bridge between the indoor and outdoor spaces, is also a feature of the living area below, particularly when people move around the apartment. The kitchen, which is open to the living areas, is defined by the lower ceiling height. Keeping the design as simple as possible, the kitchen was designed as one continuous line against the wall.

Even though the bedrooms upstairs do not have floor-to-ceiling windows, like the living areas, they do benefit from a massive window wall, drawing in the light and the views. As an alternative to a window in one of the bedrooms upstairs, the wall was cut away, leaving the built-in drawers to create both storage and the necessary privacy.

While the interiors are captivating, it is the copper façade that slows down the traffic outside. The massing and materials of the southern façade work to mediate, on an urban design level, between the four-storey apartment building to the west and the three-storey heritage building to the east. It was a matter of respecting the smaller scale buildings. That same respect and understanding of small spaces is clearly apparent within their own apartments.

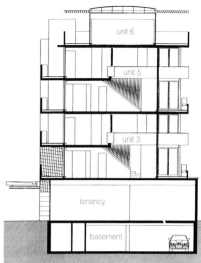

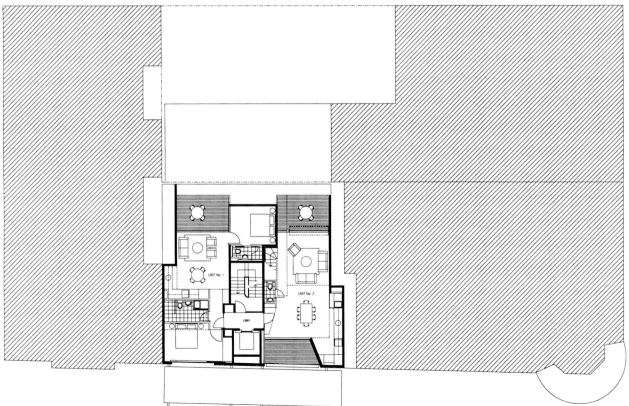

# A NEW RHYTHM

## DANIEL VAN CLEEMPUT

Photography: John Gollings

Surrounded by Victorian terraces, this inner city home wasn't designed to duplicate its neighbours. Instead of Victorian shaped windows, a cedar façade with a band of windows commencing at door height was created.

For the owner, an artist, the band of high windows across the façade allows the front room to be used as a studio. The back door of the steel letterbox, which features on the studio wall, is a reminder of the home's street frontage. While the front room is used for a studio, it could equally be a living area or double as a guest bedroom. When architect Daniel Van Cleemput drew up plans for the house, on a site measuring only 3.6 metres wide by 16 metres in depth, the rooms were numbered rather than labelled. 'I knew how my client wanted to use the spaces, but I was mindful that he didn't want to feel restricted. The three open areas could be used for sleeping or for extra living space. The only internal door in the whole house is for the bathroom', Van Cleemput says.

The kitchen, which acts as the functional core on the first level, conceals the utilities. Hidden behind the hoop pine cupboards, under the stairs, is the washing machine. In the same way, many of the kitchen's appliances are tucked away behind the floor-to-ceiling cupboards. For Van Cleemput, who worked as an architect in Belgium for many years, the small dimensions of the site were familiar. 'One of the problems with sites like this is getting natural light into the centre. Having the kitchen elevated allows for greater light', he says.

The two rooms on the first floor are used as a bedroom and living area. However, the living area is often used as a second studio or bedroom. The main bedroom, which faces west, takes in the rooftops of neighbouring terraces. To create privacy, Van Cleemput lined the balcony with floor-to-ceiling cedar battens. 'The rear façade was designed in a series of layers. There's the cedar screen, the brace of the building and the steel grate flooring of the balcony. It creates a sense of transparency', Van Cleemput explains.

The steel grate staircase that leads to the rooftop terrace allows the sunlight to filter into the lower levels of the home. The top level was designed as a lantern with its corrugated fibreglass canopy and wall. As the light increases on every level, so do the views over the terraces below. As Van Cleemput says, 'I treated the particle board on the first floor as though it were parquetry. It was given the same three coats of lacquer. Even if the budget was twice as large, I would still like to think that I would come up with the same design'.

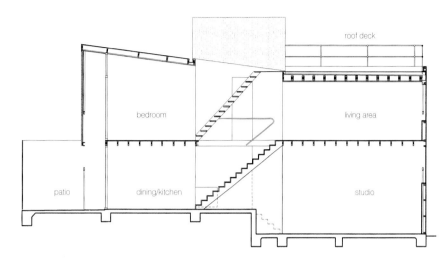

roof deck

bedroom                    living area

patio    dining/kitchen    studio

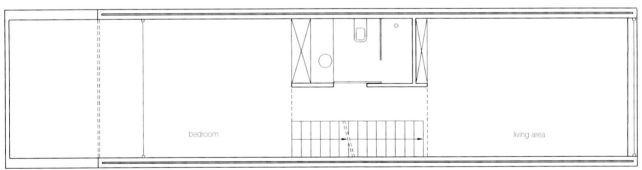

bedroom

living area

# REINVENTING A COTTAGE
## WHITING ARCHITECTURE + INTERIORS
### Photography: Trevor Mein

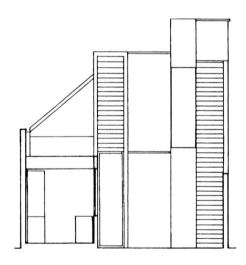

From the street this cottage, with its steeply pitched roof, appears no more than a few rooms deep. When architect Steven Whiting first inspected the cottage, it was not the number of rooms that concerned him, but the internal arrangement. 'There was no outlook. It was a strange collection of windows and doors', Whiting says.

As the site was small, Whiting was keen to develop as much space as possible into the pitched roof. 'It is a heritage area so I had to retain the front façade', he says. Instead of thinking of the space as a series of floor plans, Whiting approached the design as though it were a piece of sculpture. 'I approached the design as though I were carving spaces out of the volume. It was treated as a three-dimensional space not as a series of flat plans'. Instead of a narrow corridor, the entrance reveals a three-level home. 'It looks like a series of boxes inserted into the space, with the stairs acting as the spine to all the rooms. It is almost an atrium lobby in a miniature form', Whiting says. With the bathroom door adjacent to the entrance and designed with a frosted glass wall, the space appears significantly larger.

The main bedroom, on the first floor, was inserted into the pitched roofline, while the third level was given over to the home office. The robes and ensuite are also tucked into the roof space, extending to become a storage area when the ceiling height diminishes. As space was limited in the kitchen and living areas on the ground floor, Whiting included a built-in seating area against the large paned window. 'There is quite a lot of seating in the living area without bringing in massive lounges. Placed against the window, this area attracts the elements, such as the morning summer sunlight', Whiting says. While the galley-style kitchen is elongated, Whiting used a cherry wood splashback to accentuate what depth was available. 'Basically the shell is white. I used timber flooring, glass and stone to accentuate the warmth', he says.

As every metre counted on site, the design was cantilevered into the rear yard. The 'floating' rectangular shape provides extra storage for the main bedroom upstairs. 'The envelope was pushed to its maximum. Originally the cottage was only about 75 metres square. We probably doubled that amount of space with the renovation', Whiting says. 'The site is still only six metres in width. It is the volume that has doubled. The views have also multiplied. From the study you can now see views of the city'.

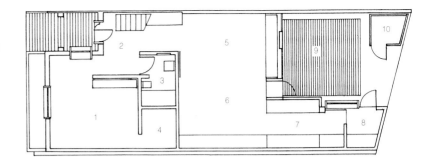

1 Nursery
2 Entry
3 Bathroom
4 Walk-in-robe
5 Living
6 Dining
7 Kitchen
8 Laundry
9 Decking
10 Shed

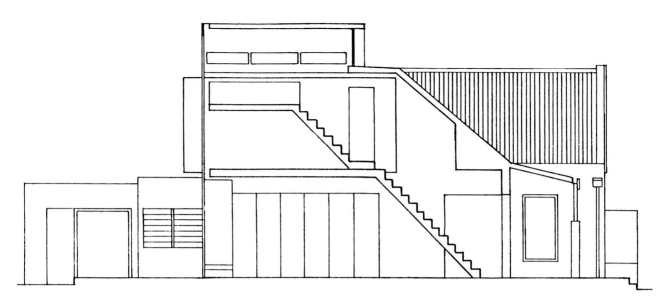

# Down
# a Laneway

## WILLIAM ORR

Photography: Andrew Iser

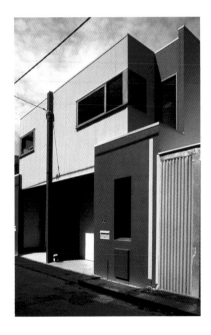

This townhouse, designed by architect William Orr, is located down a laneway. Nestled behind an old Victorian home, the site was subdivided to create these two new townhouses. The laneway, with its mixture of warehouses and cottages, shows a different side to the street.

The two new townhouses, which feature colour-bond cladding and rendered brickwork, create a new layer to the laneway's development. Apart from the sense of discovery, the lane provides an alternative to the traditional street frontage. 'Those who want to live in the inner areas and are finding the cost prohibitive should start looking at developments in the lanes', says Orr.

The two-bedroom townhouse, which includes an open plan kitchen, is loosely defined with a minimal amount of joinery. 'It is a fairly undefined kitchen. It functions as another living space. I also included polished concrete floors in the garage. When the car is not there it can be used for a studio', he says. As there wasn't the large backyard to call on, Orr was careful to dissolve the boundaries of the living spaces. 'I used the Chinese landscape concept of the 'borrowed landscape'. It's important to look beyond the building and to utilise the distant landscape to create the illusion of space', Orr says.

For the owner, Bill Robertson, a landscape architect, restoring a large old house every weekend had little appeal. 'When I first came through this townhouse, all I could notice was how spacious and light it was. With high fences designed around the place, there is no one peeping into your back garden', he says. 'The aural sensations become more acute when you are living in a dynamic environment. You might not have a view over a rolling front lawn but there is a continual reminder of where you are', Robertson says.

When the project is small, the detail often becomes more crucial. 'For this home, the cupboard joinery details were recessed to make the doors part of the plane of the walls. It is only a minor detail, but it adds to the feeling of space', Orr says.

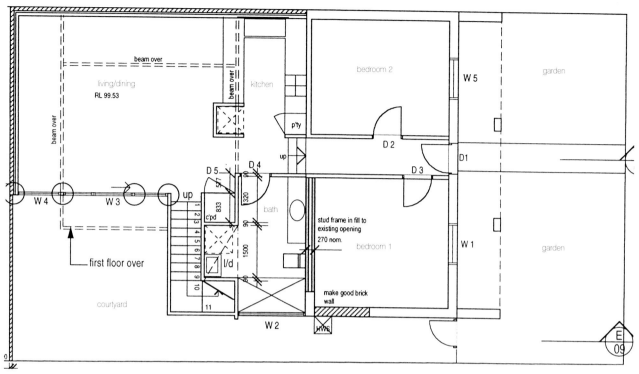

beam over

living/dining
RL 99.53

beam over

beam over

kitchen

p'ty

up

bedroom 2

W 5

garden

D 2

D 5

D 4

90

90

577

320

1500

833

c'pd

l/d

bath

D 3

D1

D 3

stud frame in fill to
existing opening
270 nom.

bedroom 1

W 1

garden

W 4

W 3

up

1
2
3
4
5
6
7
8
9
10
11

first floor over

courtyard

make good brick
wall

W 2

HWS

E
09

0

173

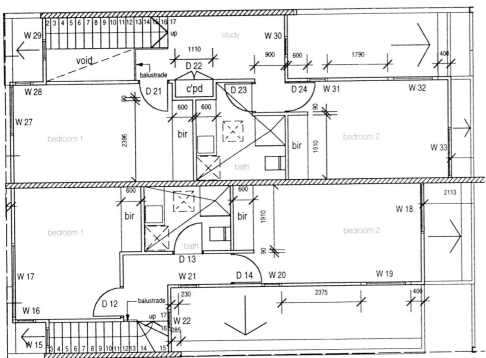

## ACKNOWLEDGMENTS

I would like to thank all the architects featured in this book, for turning the word small into something much larger. Thanks must also go to the many photographers who contributed. Like the architects and designers who cleverly manipulated the spaces, the photographers have created a much larger vision. I would especially like to thank my partner, Naomi, for her support, constructive comments and patience. Some of the work shown has appeared in the Melbourne *Age* newspaper.